Chris C. Pinney, D.V.M.

German Shorthaired Pointers

Everything about Purchase, Care,
Nutrition, Breeding, Behavior,
and Training

With 51 Color Photographs

Illustrations by Erin O'Toole

BARRON'S

About the Author

Chris C. Pinney, DVM is a practicing veterinarian from Schulenburg, Texas. He has authored six books pertaining to pets, including *Guide to Home Pet Grooming*, *Caring for Your Older Dog*, and the award-winning *Caring for Your Older Cat*, by Barron's Educational Series, Inc.

Photo Credits

Barbara Augello: front cover, page 65 bottom; Mike Ross: inside front cover, pages 25, 32, 37, 40, 45, 49, 53, 64 top, 64 bottom, 65 top, 73, 76 bottom, 77, 81, 85, 88, 89 top, 89 bottom, inside back cover, back cover; Bob Schwartz: pages 4 top, 9, 21, 33, 48, 80, 84 bottom, 97, 100; Judith Strom: pages 4 bottom, 5, 8, 13 bottom, 76 top, 93; Bonnie Nance: pages 12, 13 top, 17, 20, 24, 56, 60, 84 top; Zig Leszczynski: pages 16, 36, 41, 68; Toni Tucker: page 101.

© Copyright 1998 by Chris C. Pinney, DVM

All inquiries should be addressed to:
Barron's Educational Series, Inc.
250 Wireless Boulevard
Hauppauge, NY 11788
http://www.barronseduc.com

International Standard Book No. 0-7641-0316-4

Library of Congress Catalog Card No. 97-44383

Library of Congress Cataloging-in-Publication Data
Pinney, Chris C.
    German shorthaired pointers : a complete pet owner's manual / by Chris C. Pinney
        p.   cm.
    Includes bibliographical references (p.   ) and index.
    ISBN 0-7641-0316-4
    1. German shorthaired pointer. I. Title.
SF429.G4P55   1998
636.752′5—dc21   97-44383
                                             CIP

Printed in China

987

Important Note
Always use caution and common sense whenever handling a dog, especially one that may be ill or injured. Employ proper restraint devices as necessary. In addition, if the information and procedures contained in this book differ in any way from your veterinarian's recommendations concerning your pet's health care, please consult him/her prior to their implementation. Finally, because each pet is unique, always consult your veterinarian before administering any type of treatment or medication to your pet.

Contents

The German Shorthaired Pointer is the most popular general utility gun dog in the United States.

German Shorthaired Pointers are at home in the outdoors.

Introduction

The German Shorthaired Pointer is by far the most popular general utility gun dog found in North America today. In the United States alone, well over 10,000 of them are registered with the American Kennel Club each year. This general utility group includes those breeds that can locate, point, and retrieve game, all with moderate to excellent efficiency. Along with German Shorthaired Pointers, Vizslas, Weimaraners, German Wirehaired Pointers, and Brittanies fall under this category as well.

Highly intelligent, with an incredibly strong desire to please their owners, German Shorthaired Pointers are known for their gentle dispositions and affectionate natures. Not only do they make great all-around gun dogs, but they make great household companions too!

As hunters, German Shorthaired Pointers rank among the most adaptable of breeds. They can be found hunting all across the United States, whether it be ruffed grouse in Michigan, woodcock in Minnesota, pheasant in Nebraska, bobwhite quail in Texas, ducks in North Carolina, or rabbits in Pennsylvania. Equipped with a dominant pointing instinct and armed with an excellent nose and scenting ability, the German Shorthaired Pointer can track down all types of game in all types of conditions and terrains. It can be a skillful retriever as well, especially if game has fallen into heavy cover or thicket. When given a chance, German Shorthaired Pointers will take to the water without hesitation. They are excellent swimmers, aided by their thick, short haircoats that provide buoyancy.

As a rule, German Shorthairs tend to have a closer hunting range than do their pointer and setter counterparts. This makes them ideal for conditions where dense cover and wooded areas exist. It is no wonder that they are such a favorite for hunting upland game birds such as ruffed grouse, woodcock, and partridge.

These durable dogs tend to hunt at a much slower pace than their English or Continental cousins, which allows them to conserve energy during the hunt. As a result, shorthairs will often go much longer without tiring and will exhibit much more stamina on the hunt than other hunting dogs. For the hunter on foot, this slower pace makes for a relaxed, unhurried hunt.

Retrieving a chukar.

The versatile German Shorthaired Pointer is used to hunt a variety of upland game birds.

As mentioned above, German Shorthaired Pointers are employed to hunt a wide variety of game. Being a multipurpose hunter, its expertise with various types of game can vary. For instance, hunting pheasant in corn fields or grasslands can challenge the Shorthair, owing to the fact that today's pheasant tends to stay on

Swimming comes naturally to most Shorthairs.

the ground more, preferring to run rather than take to flight. Because of their hound ancestry, German Shorthaired Pointers will often lean more toward tracking game via foot scent rather than aerial scent. As a result, if the pheasant are running, nonproductive or false points can occur (see page 84). Does this mean that German Shorthaired Pointers shouldn't be used to hunt pheasant? On the contrary, with experience, training, and patience, the German Shorthaired Pointer can become a highly effective tool to locate and hold ring-necked pheasants.

In contrast to the ring-necked pheasant, ruffed grouse and partridge are close ranging birds that would rather take to flight than run. As a result, this makes them ideal game for the Shorthair. The same holds true for woodcock. These birds will sit tight and freeze when a dog approaches. Since they are found in dense, thicket areas, you need a dog that is not afraid to enter such terrain. The German Shorthaired Pointer fits this description to a tee!

German Shorthaired Pointers are also ideal for hunting quail situated in small, compact fields with dense hedge rows and thickets. Quail located in large open fields can prove to be a more difficult quarry to hunt due to the slower hunting pace of the Shorthair and the broader range that must be covered, but rest assured that it won't be the dog who runs out of energy first when hunting in such conditions!

Finally, these Teutonic hunters are excellent at retrieving upland game birds that have fallen into water. However, understand that they were not bred to brave extremely cold water for extended periods of time. As a result, cold-water duck hunting can test even the toughest of Shorthairs. Also, because of their high energy levels and desire to be in motion, German

Shorthairs often gets restless and agitated when made to sit in or next to a blind. This does not, however, discount them from performing this function effectively. Again, with training and experience, they can certainly give their retriever friends a run for their money!

As pets, German Shorthaired Pointers are wonderful. Their disposition is such that they make affectionate companions, and are especially lovable around children. Although their nature is naturally gentle and easy going, rest assured they can become formidable protectors if they feel any members of their pack are threatened.

These dogs are especially responsive to the authority of their trainers or owners, which in itself has a highly positive influence on the bonding that occurs between owner and dog, and upon the training process. Rarely do they get their feelings hurt when reprimanded. When they do, they seem to bounce back and recapture their positive attitudes quite rapidly.

By nature, this is a very energetic and active breed, and as such, Shorthairs need to be able to expend built-

German Shorthaired Pointers can be excellent retrievers as well.

up energy several times a day. Because they like to move, they may not do particularly well in apartment or townhouse settings, or in small kennel enclosures, in which space to run is limited. They need space: Space to run, play, point, and unleash their instinctive desires for the hunt!

The History of the Breed

To trace the history and ancestry of this remarkable breed, one must travel back through history to nineteenth century Europe. The rise of the German Empire under Prussian leadership was in full swing during the mid 1800s. For the first time, the army, which up to this time had been manned chiefly by the Prussian aristocracy and peasantry, was opened up to the middle class. This, combined with sweeping economic and political changes occurring throughout Europe, led to a rise in the status of the middle class within the Empire. With this rise came increased privileges with regard to land ownership and hunting. Understand that in previous centuries, it was usually only the kings, princes, and nobles who possessed the right to hunt, and the same people owned vast tracts of land for this purpose. However, as the wealth of middle class Prussia grew during the 1800s, merchants, professionals, and other middle-class citizens were able to purchase or lease land for themselves on which, of course, they could hunt.

In Germany, dense forests blended with open fields and housed all types of feather and fur, including grouse, rabbit, fox, deer, wolves, and wild boar. It was there that a desire arose within the hearts of Teutonic hunters to create a breed of hunting dog that could effectively hunt all types of game in all types of terrain that their homeland had to offer. They wanted a dog with a nose sensitive enough to locate game at an acceptable, useful distance. Since the German hunter typically hunted on foot, they also wanted a dog that had enough discipline and inbred instinct to remain staunch on point once the game was located to allow them ample time to close in on the quarry. A hunting partner was needed that would retrieve fallen game for them both on land and in water. In addition, the dog needed to be bold and aggressive enough to interact with and track larger game such as wild cats, foxes and deer within the deep German forests. Finally, and very importantly, these hunters wanted a household companion that could be relied upon to protect the home and those within it effectively when called upon to do so.

German Shorthairs are at home in all types of terrain.

Keeping all of these qualities in mind, the seed of this dream was effectively planted, and the work was begun to develop such a dog.

Many different theories exist regarding the actual origins and ancestry of the German Shorthaired Pointer, but most experts believe that the breed development was initiated by a cross between the old Spanish Pointer and traditional continental pointers, including the German Pointer and French Braque. German hunters decided to further cross the breed with tracking hounds such as the German bloodhound and French Gascon to further enhance scenting ability and to soften the temperament of the emerging breed. The genes of these German tracking hounds also helped to overcome many of the unwanted or undesirable characteristics of the traditional Pointers, including reduced trailing ability, a natural aversion to water work, and a noted lack of aggressiveness toward predators. Yet even with all these improvements, early breeders were still not satisfied. The dogs that were created from the previous crosses were proving to be too slow in the hunt and lacking in true agility. In addition, these hunters liked the scenting prowess that came from the bloodhound, yet didn't want their new breed to look like a bloodhound. As a result, during the 1860s, still another cross was made with the English Pointer to improve the speed, style, looks, and pointing instincts of the breed. The end product of all of these efforts was a sleek, good-looking, intelligent, loyal, and versatile gun dog with incredible stamina, an acute sense of smell, a highly developed pointing instinct, and an eagerness to retrieve fallen game either on land or in water. Now the German hunter had a companion that could trail and scent both furred and feathered game, could point and retrieve game birds, and had the size, strength,

and courage to interact with larger game such as deer, fox, and boar. These dogs were real performers.

In 1872, the first German Shorthaired Pointer made its way into the German Kennel Club Stud Book. His name: Hektor I ZK I. Eleven years later, two German Shorthairs named "Nero" and "Treff" competed against each other in the German Derby of 1883. As it turned out, both would end up becoming great foundation dogs for the breed (Nero's daughter "Flora" would later produce three offspring named "Walden," "Waldo," and "Hertha," all of whom can be credited with laying the foundation of

The hound ancestry of the German Shorthair affords it exceptional tracking skills.

many of the great pedigree lines we see today).

The popularity of the new breed soon spread across the European continent. England was slow to accept the breed's popularity, owing to the fact that much of the hunting done in that island nation was accomplished on horseback and in open fields. This type of hunting required a dog with a much broader range and speed than the German Shorthaired Pointer could provide. In addition, national pride in the English pointing breeds undoubtedly contributed to this slow acceptance of the German Shorthaired Pointer. In 1887, the German Shorthaired Pointer did appear on exhibit in England at the Barns Elms Show. However, its introduction was short lived, and German Shorthaired Pointers were not seen with regularity in Britain until after the Second World War. The breed's popularity continued to flourish on the Continent, and in

A Prussian officer with his Shorthair companions.

1891, the Klub Kurzhaar was founded for the purpose of maintaining the standards and guidelines for this new and exciting type of sporting dog.

In 1925, Dr. Charles Thorton of Missoula, Montana, a physician and staunch upland game hunter, introduced an Austrian female German Shorthaired Pointer named "Senta von Hohenbruch" into the United States. At the time, she came from the top of the German-Austrian bloodline of German Shorthaired Pointers, as did many of those that followed. Although it is probable that a number of German Shorthaired Pointers entered America with German immigrant masters prior to 1925, Dr. Thorton is rightly given credit as being the "father" of the breed in the United States and was instrumental in increasing awareness of the breed across America. Initially, skepticism concerning the breed's abilities slowed the growth of this popularity. However, the German Shorthair soon proved itself as a formidable hunter and became a very popular dog with American hunters, who, like their German counterparts, enjoyed hunting on foot. In 1930, the breed was recognized by the American Kennel Club (AKC), with "Grief v.d. Fliegerhalde" becoming the first German Shorthaired Pointer registered with the organization. The first national AKC-licensed specialty show was held in 1941 at the International Kennel Club show in Chicago, Illinois. Field trials emerged in 1944, the first being an AKC-licensed event held in Minnesota by the German Shorthaired Pointer Club of America. This club today is the AKC Parent Club and official sponsor of the breed in the United States. Promoting the German Shorthaired Pointer's popularity as a versatile hunter, the German Shorthaired Pointer Club of America has built a solid foundation for the breed and its development for years to come.

Selecting Your German Shorthaired Pointer

Before choosing the Shorthair that's just right for you, there are a number of factors you need to consider. For starters, is your German Shorthaired Pointer going to simply be a house pet or show dog, or are you planning on utilizing it as a hunting dog? Your answer to this question certainly has a direct bearing on the selection process.

German Shorthaired Pointers as Pets

Although German Shorthairs were originally developed for hunting, you don't have to be a hunter to experience the pleasure and companionship that this breed can bring to you. As mentioned previously, German Shorthaired Pointers are highly affectionate and loving dogs, and bond closely to their owners. Loyal to the core, you can count on yours being at your side every chance it gets! These dogs are smart and easily trainable, which is a big plus for the owner who may not have a lot of time to devote to training. They are also eager to please, a plus for those owners aspiring to enter competitive show events. The Shorthair's size and body structure, as well as inherent instincts, makes it an excellent watchdog and protector of the family. For fitness buffs, Shorthairs are built for endurance and stamina, making them super exercise partners for walkers and runners.

Still another reason many persons choose the German Shorthaired Pointer for a pet is that it is a relatively low maintenance dog. Shorthairs harbor very few psychological vices if given adequate attention. The breed as a whole is sturdy and healthy due to a large and diverse ancestral gene pool. Shorthairs are clean dogs, with short haircoats that make routine grooming a relatively easy process. In addition, their teeth accumulate tartar at a seemingly slower pace than those of smaller breeds. While this latter fact may seem trivial, it is in fact quite important when you consider the positive impact that good dental health can have on the length and quality of life of a dog, as well as the expenses associated with preventive dental care programs.

As with any breed, idiosyncrasies do exist that you need to be aware of if considering the Shorthair as a pet. To begin, these dogs are bundles of energy packed in large frames and as such, need lots of exercise and attention daily. Shorthairs that aren't allowed to vent this energy are highly prone to boredom and frustration, which in turn can lead to behavioral challenges and compulsive behavior. Also, pointers that are housed outdoors away from the presence of their owners are also more prone to develop bad behaviors, including nuisance barking, self-mutilation (i.e., psychotic chewing and scratching), and digging. Thirdly, owing to their size, German Shorthaired Pointers may not be suitable selections for apartment dwellers or for those people with limited living space. In addition, this size, when combined with the

German Shorthairs love to please their owners.

playful energy that comes naturally to the breed, may make them incompatible with households containing very young children and infants. Last, but not least, before committing to any dog the size of the German Shorthaired Pointer, realize that the cost associated with feeding such a dog (and the effort expended cleaning up after one) is certainly greater than it would be if dealing with a smaller dog.

Deciding upon which sex your new Shorthair should be is strictly a matter of personal partiality. Both male and female Shorthairs make excellent pets. Male dogs tend to be more spirited and protective, whereas females are generally regarded as more affectionate and trainable. However, such qualities will vary between individual dogs, and will be influenced by factors such as genetics, training, and neutering.

All said, the German Shorthaired Pointer can make an excellent household pet, and the decision to own one is a matter of personal preference and circumstance. Rest assured that you will be gaining a loyal, loving companion. Just be sure to give your new companion the attention it deserves (and needs) on a daily basis!

Selecting the Hunting Dog

If you are planning to use your dog for hunting purposes, there are several points to consider in the selection process. The first is whether you want a fully-trained mature hunting dog or an untrained puppy or adolescent. This decision should be influenced by the time you will have available to devote to training, the confidence you have in your ability to do the training, the extent of actual training and refinement you desire for your dog, and finally, the amount of money you are willing to spend on the process.

Purchasing an untrained puppy affords you the opportunity to closely bond with it during its peak socialization period, which occurs between eight and twelve weeks of age. In addition, you will be able to experience the satisfaction of transforming an inexperienced puppy into a trained bird dog and/or companion. Still another advantage of purchasing an untrained puppy is cost; its price tag is considerably less than that of a partially or fully-trained German Shorthaired Pointer. The disadvantage, of course, of purchasing an untrained puppy is the time required to mold it into a functional hunter. You also run the risk of training mistakes, many of which might be avoided by professional training.

The advantages of purchasing a trained dog are numerous and many experts feel that these advantages far outweigh any disadvantages that may exist with this option. Purchasing a trained dog can save you anywhere

A six week old Shorthair puppy on point.

from one to three years of time, a real benefit if you consider what your time is worth. Your risk of training mistakes is greatly minimized and the chances of getting a dog with serious behavioral or physical problems is virtually eliminated. In addition, a trained dog offers you immediate gratification and benefits that you can put to use almost immediately.

Purchasing a fully-trained Shorthair allows you to enjoy the benefits immediately.

13

Table 2: Factors to Consider Prior to Purchasing a German Shorthaired Pointer

- Age (Puppy; Young Adult; Adult)
- Sex (Male versus Female; Neutered versus Intact)
- Source (Local breeder; Out-of-town; Mail Order)
- Expenses Associated With Ownership (Food; Veterinary; Training; Competitions)
- Prior Training (None; Started; Fully Trained)
- Housing (Indoors versus Outdoors)

As mentioned earlier, the biggest disadvantage of purchasing a trained dog is cost. Fully-trained Shorthairs can cost three to four times as much as untrained pups, depending upon the level of training received.

There are two types of trained gun dogs you can choose from. The first, most experienced level, is the "fully-trained" dog. Fully-trained Shorthairs should be able to remain staunch on point, respond to basic obedience commands, and have an inner excitement and zeal for the hunt. Most of these dogs will be one and a half to three years of age at the time of purchase. The other type of trained dog you can obtain is one that has been "started." Started dogs will exhibit the same characteristics as fully-trained dogs, yet may not exhibit staunchness on point (see Remaining Staunch on Point, page 84). Most started dogs will be between the ages of one and two years at time of purchase. Neither fully-trained nor started gun dogs should be expected to be trained in steadiness to wing and shot or to retrieve.

The type of range restrictions placed on the dog during its training is an important factor worthy of inquiry. As a rule, the majority of German Shorthaired Pointers are trained to be close to

medium-range workers (10 to 75 yards). However, be sure you find out the range at which your dog was trained.

Another decision you need to make is whether your new hunting dog will be a male or a female. As mentioned previously, this is strictly a matter of personal preference. Both sexes offer distinct advantages and disadvantages as hunters. For instance, male German Shorthaired Pointers are believed to exhibit extra drive and stamina during the hunt, whereas females have gained the reputation for being more biddable, loving, and responsive. One definite factor you will have to contend with if you choose a female is her heat cycle. On the average, female German Shorthaired Pointers come into heat twice yearly, and there is always a chance that a heat cycle could coincide with hunting season. Although she still will hunt, hormonal influences during this time could adversely affect her performance. In addition, she obviously could not be hunted alongside male dogs during her heat cycle without causing a distraction. Of course, if you are not planning on breeding her, having her spayed will eliminate these concerns altogether.

Finding the German Shorthaired Pointer That's Just Right for You

So where do you begin your search for your German Shorthaired Pointer? A good place to start is your local or national breed association. It should be able to direct you to a number of reputable breeders and/or trainers who may have the dog you have been looking for. Dog trainers, hunting clubs, and shooting preserves can provide a wealth of information as well. In addition, most sporting journals, hunting magazines, and dog-related publications are full of information and advertisements for trained and untrained gun dogs, as well as

Shorthairs that would make great house pets and show dogs.

When purchasing your Shorthair, be sure to request a copy of the dog's pedigree, including the AKC registration certification papers of its parents. If feasible, go to the breeder's location to observe and interact with the puppy or dog in its original environment. When trying to decide on one, look closely at the personality of each. The dog or puppy you'll want to choose should not be shy and hesitant to interact with you, nor should it be too overbearing and rambunctious. Your final selection should have a personality that falls somewhere in between these two extremes.

If it is not possible to pick out your dog in person, request a 30-day trial period, prior to the payment of any money, in which you can test your dog's personality and temperament, not to mention its hunting skills if it is already trained (if you are planning on purchasing a trained dog, coordinate your purchase to coincide as closely with hunting season as possible so that your new dog's performance can be evaluated immediately). For dogs purchased via mail order, this may mean paying to have the dog shipped out to you; however, this is a small investment, considering what is at stake! Most reputable breeders and trainers stand behind the quality of their dogs and rarely have a problem with such an arrangement. If the dog proves to be unsatisfactory for any reason, most will allow you to return it (at your expense, of course) with no questions asked.

If you are planning to show your German Shorthaired Pointer, be sure to select a dog with a championship pedigree. Of course, such a selection will come with a higher price tag, but if you are serious about competing, it will no doubt help give you and your dog the edge needed to beat the competition in the show ring.

Upon the purchase of your dog, its breeder will give you an AKC registration application, which has been partially filled out with information pertaining to your dog's characteristics, pedigree, and date of birth. Finish filling out this form with your name, address, and the name you would like your dog registered under (see below), and mail it and the application fee directly to the American Kennel Club. The AKC will then send you an official registration certificate for your safekeeping.

Bringing Your New German Shorthaired Pointer Home

Prior to bringing your new German Shorthaired Pointer home, you'll want to do everything in your power to make your new friend feel comfortable and secure in its new surroundings. Some minor planning on your part can make the transition much easier for it. Table 3 contains a handy checklist of items you'll need to purchase prior to your dog's arrival. Also, be sure to decide upon who in the family is going to be responsible for daily feedings, brushing, dental care, training, etc. for the new addition. Remember: If it doesn't get assigned, you don't need to guess who will end up doing it all.

Provide your dog with a comfortable place to bed down.

Housing Considerations

There is a general myth about housing hunting dogs that deserves to be laid to rest here and now. Some old-timers insist that a hunting dog's place is in the backyard in a kennel; that keeping it inside will make it soft and ruin its hunting prowess. Nothing could be further from the truth! A properly trained German Shorthaired Pointer makes an excellent indoor dog; in fact, one of the many functions that this breed was developed for was as that of family protector within a dwelling. In addition, because dogs are by nature pack animals, dogs housed indoors with their pack tend to be more emotionally stable than dogs isolated by themselves outside.

If you are planning to house your German Shorthaired Pointer indoors, it will need a special area or room that it can claim as its den and sleeping quarters. When you first get a puppy home, the first place you should introduce it to is this area. Allow the pup 15 minutes or so to scope out the area prior to allowing it into the rest of the home. Make the experience a pleasurable one! Praise your puppy enthusiastically and offer it some food to eat. Get it to associate that location with ultimate pleasure. If you are bringing a newly purchased adult German Shorthaired Pointer into the house, be sure to ask the breeder where the dog slept while in his care

Naming your new addition should be a family event.

and consider allowing your dog access to a similar location in your house.

When keeping a dog (and especially a puppy) indoors, there are a number of safety measures you should implement within your house to ensure an accident-free environment for your pet. First, keep all plants out of reach. Puppies love to chew on plants, and could harm themselves if they ingest a poisonous variety. Keep all electrical cords well out of reach. This may mean banishing your playful pet from certain areas of the house, but this is a minor inconvenience compared to a potentially fatal accident. Again, puppies love to chew, and electrical cords are mighty appetizing to unrefined tastes. Keep everything that's not a dog toy picked up, including spare change. Pennies contain high levels of zinc, and could cause a severe gastroenteritis if swallowed. Remember:

Puppies explore their environments with their mouths, and will pick up (and often eat) anything.

Table 3: Supplies Needed for Your New German Shorthaired Pointer
- Bristle Brush
- Dentifrice
- Ear Cleanser
- First-aid Kit (see Table 5 page 50)
- Food and Water Bowls
- Identification Tags
- Leash
- Leather or Nylon Collar
- Nail Trimmers/Styptic Powder
- Premium Dog Food (Puppy Food)
- Sleeping Quarters (Bed, Travel Kennel, and/or Doghouse)
- Toys/Chew Bones
- Training Items (see Table 7 page 78)
- Travel Kennel

Electrical cords can be lethal hazards to young puppies.

Obviously, you'll want to confine your German Shorthaired Pointer to non-carpeted floors until it's properly housetrained (see page 74). Even so-called "stain-resistant" carpets may not uphold this claim after repeated bombardments.

There will undoubtedly be special situations that prohibit the indoor dwelling of a grown dog. In these instances, outdoor accommodations provided for your pet must take into account its comfort and well-being. Remember that dogs get hot and cold just like we do, and when housed outdoors, they need to be provided a means of protection against extremes in the weather. Your German Shorthaired Pointer is entitled to a sturdy, well-insulated shelter. It should be positioned in a relatively shady area of the yard, and should also be elevated a few inches off of the ground using bricks or wood to prevent flooding in the event of a rain storm. Ideally, the shelter should have a short, enclosed porch that leads into the main house. This will help keep wind drafts from penetrating into the main living area. The main living quarters should be large enough to allow your dog to turn around comfortably, yet confined enough to provide it a sense of security and to concentrate heat during cold winter days. Finally, a ramp should be included to allow your dog

easy access into its abode, especially after a long day's hunt.

If you wish to build the house yourself, select sturdy building materials, remembering that they may need to be able to withstand constant punishment from teeth and claws. If fiberglass insulation is to be used, make certain it remains well-contained and sealed within the walls and roof, since such material can cause severe gastrointestinal upset if swallowed.

If you plan on further confining your dog to a pen or run, use a smooth concrete or quarry tile as flooring for the enclosure. Though such surfaces may not be the most comfortable for your pet, they are the most sanitary and easy to clean. Floors consisting of grass, sand, pebbles, and/or just plain dirt only serve to trap and accumulate filth and disease, and should be avoided.

The fence surrounding the enclosure should be made of wire chain link and be tall enough to prevent an acrobatic exit. Exposed metal points from the chain links at the top of the fencing material should not be allowed to extend above the metal support bar, to prevent injuries if your dog does try to jump. The same rule applies for the bottom perimeter of the fence as well, just in case your dog tries to squeeze its way out from down under.

Keep in mind that daily interaction with and attention given to your outdoor dog is essential to both its mental and physical health, especially for the dog that was raised indoors as a puppy. As a responsible pet owner, you owe it to your friend!

Naming Your New Dog

Naming your new addition should be fun and involve the entire family. You can even find entire books dedicated to choosing the right name for your dog at your favorite bookstore. Stick to names having two syllables; this will allow your dog easy differentiation between its name and those one syllable commands that it will learn during obedience and field training. You can further set its name apart by adding a vowel sound to the end of it. Be consistent when using the name. If you name your dog "Nifta," don't shorten it on occasion to "Nif." You'll only confuse your pet as to its true identity.

First Encounters

If you purchased a puppy, its first encounters with your family members are important. Be sure that the initial introductions, be they with children or other adults in the family, turn out to be positive ones. Carefully supervise children–pet interactions and stress the importance of gentle play and handling. Instruct your children and other adults on the proper way to pick up and hold the new puppy. Dogs should not be picked up solely by the front legs or by the neck; instead, the entire body should be picked up as one unit, with the hind end supported, not left dangling in mid-air.

If they had it their way, most children, and some adults for that matter, would love to play with a new puppy 24 hours out of the day. You need to stress the importance of rest times for their new puppy after periods of play, and lay strict ground rules against disturbing it while it is in its special room or bed. It is fine to play hard with your puppy, but overt rough-housing should be avoided. If a play session progresses from a friendly romp to an all out frontal assault, end it immediately. Your puppy needs to learn how to control its activity level to an intensity that is socially acceptable. The same applies to chewing. It's perfectly natural for a puppy to want to explore its environment and express itself with its mouth. During play there will be times when it will bite and nip; when this occurs, simply and strongly say "No,"

Make sure your puppy's first encounters with you and its new home are nothing but positive.

and provide a chew toy as a substitute. Remember that if you are planning to train a hunter, avoid playing any type of "tug-of-war" with your puppy. Doing so only creates a dog with a "hard mouth" when it comes to retrieving birds.

Toys that you purchase for your new Shorthair to play with should be made of nylon, rawhide, or hard rubber. Of the three, the first is most desirable, since it is most easily digestible if swallowed. Rawhides are fine if the dog takes its time and chews slowly. For gulpers or engulfers who don't have time for chewing, avoid giving rawhides, which can cause serious stomach upset and sometimes intestinal blockages if swallowed whole. Also, some dogs

To prevent destructive chewing, provide your new puppy with plenty of toys and chewing devices.

have difficulty differentiating rawhide from leather, which could put a new pair of shoes in serious jeopardy. Rubber chew toys should be solid so as not to be easily ripped apart by sharp puppy teeth. Avoid chew toys with plastic "squeaks" in them. These can be easily extracted by most dogs, and can be swallowed or aspirated all too easily. Regardless of the type of chew toy you pick, choose it as you would a toy for a child. If its design is such that it could cause suffocation or serious problems if swallowed, put it back and choose a safer one.

Avoid using old socks, shoes, or sweatshirts as substitute toys for your Shorthair. It can't tell the difference between old and new. Allow a puppy to chew on an old shoe or sweatshirt while still an adolescent, and you may find it fancying your expensive leather shoes or tennis warm-ups when it grows up.

Preventive Health Care for Your German Shorthaired Pointer

Have you ever heard the old cliché "An ounce of prevention is worth a pound of cure?" Well, this is certainly the case when it comes to your gun dog. A thorough preventive and maintenance health-care plan is essential for maintaining a high standard of health and quality of life for your companion. Focus areas in a well-balanced preventive health-care program for your German Shorthaired Pointer include at-home physical examinations, vaccinations, internal parasite control, external parasite control, grooming, dental care, nutrition and weight control, exercise, neutering, and safe transportation measures.

Assessing Your Dog's Overall Condition

All German Shorthaired Pointer owners should learn how to perform a basic physical examination on their pets. Although such exams are not meant to replace routine veterinary check-ups, they are helpful for detecting minor or serious conditions in their early stages of development. For convenience, these exams can be combined with regular grooming sessions.

During your next visit to the veterinarian, he or she will probably begin with an examination of your Pointer. Watch how your veterinarian performs the exam and ask to participate in the process. Discuss your desire to learn how to do it at home. Your veterinar-

ian will undoubtedly be pleased with your interest and will be happy to help develop your skills.

Begin the exam by observing your Pointer from a distance. Observe its general appearance. Watch it move back and forth. Does it appear to be moving normally? An abnormal gait with or without limping or lameness could indicate such things as weakness, nervous system problems, or musculoskeletal problems. Dogs experiencing lameness will often dip their head in response to the pain as they walk.

Canine viral diseases are spread by close contact with infected dogs.

Table 4: Recommended Vaccination Schedule

Vaccine	Age for Initial Vaccination	Age for Second Vaccination	Age for Third Vaccination	Adult Vaccinations
Distemper	8 weeks	12 weeks	16 weeks	Every 12 months
ICH (Hepatitis)	8 weeks	12 weeks	16 weeks	Every 12 months
Parvovirus	8 weeks	12 weeks	16 weeks	Every 12 months
Parainfluenza	8 weeks	12 weeks	16 weeks	Every 12 months
Leptospirosis	12 weeks	16 weeks	—	Every 12 months
Rabies	12 weeks	1 year, 3 months	—	Every 12 months
Bordetella	12 weeks	16 weeks		Every 12 months
Lyme Disease*	12 weeks	16 weeks		Every 12 months

*Check with your veterinarian to determine if this vaccine is necessary where you live.

Does your dog stand erect and relaxed? Abnormal postures such as a wide stance with the neck extended could indicate breathing difficulties caused by heart and/or lung disease. An arching of the back is often indicative of abdominal pain. Note the position of your dog's head. A tilted head is often characteristic of a dog with an irritated or infected ear canal. A droopy head may signify depression and overall malaise.

How is your friend's attitude? Is it alert, active, and friendly, or is it lethargic, depressed, or aggressive? Sick or injured animals, especially those in pain, often show aggressive behaviors; therefore, handle them with caution. Keep in mind that normal behavior will vary among individuals and in different situations. Weakness, shortness of breath, coughing, labored breathing, and, as mentioned before, a wide-based stance could be the first signs of heart or lung problems. A pale bluish hue to the tongue signifies poor tissue oxygenation, often the result of circulation problems. If your dog shows any of the above signs, obtain a pulse by gently pressing your fingers against the upper, inner portion of a leg. Normal resting pulse for a dog ranges from 60 to 120 beats per minute. Abnormal pulse or any other signs of heart or lung problems should be reported to your veterinarian immediately.

The normal temperature range for dogs is from 99.5 to 102.2°F (37.5°C to 39°C). Excited or nervous pets may have elevated temperatures, but a temperature due to excitement should rarely exceed 103.5°F (40°C). To take your Shorthair's temperature, use a digital thermometer for safety reasons (glass thermometers can break!). Lubricate the tip and insert into its rectum. Hold it in place for two minutes or until the thermometer's audible signal is heard. If the reading is higher than 103.5°F (40°C), you should call your veterinarian for advice.

Get into the habit of weighing your dog every three months and record your readings. Unexplained weight loss or weight gain that is greater than five pounds, or a pattern of continual loss or gain, should prompt you to contact your veterinarian. Such fluctuations or patterns could signify some underlying medical disorder. German Shorthair Pointers eight years of age or older should be weighed monthly, and fluctuations in excess of three pounds in either direction should be reported to your veterinarian. Additionally, keep in mind that obesity poses the same health hazards in animals that it does in humans, and can also seriously impair the hunting ability of a bird dog. An overweight Pointer should be put on a diet and an exercise program formulated and prescribed by its veterinarian.

Vaccinations

The theory behind vaccinating any dog is to provide artificially that initial exposure to certain disease agents that have been rendered noninfective within the laboratory, thereby priming the body's immune system before exposure to the real infective agent occurs. Doing so will allow for a rapid, effective immune response if this exposure does happen, without the lag time associated with a first exposure. Vaccinations against viral diseases are vital, since, as a rule, no specific treatments exist to directly combat these agents once they gain a foothold within the dog's body.

If the bitch has been properly vaccinated prior to pregnancy, most of her pups will receive protective antibodies in their mother's milk, especially during the first 24 hours of life. These "passive" antibodies are important, since the immune system of a puppy under six weeks of age is incapable of mounting an effective response to any disease organism. Around eight weeks of age, levels of these antibodies begin to taper off, leaving the puppy to fend for itself.

If a puppy that still has adequate levels of passive antibodies present in its system gets immunized, the vaccination will be rendered ineffective. For this reason, initial vaccinations for such puppies are usually given around eight weeks of age, when levels of passive antibodies are low. Vaccination as early as six weeks of age is

indicated in those instances where the mother was not current on her vaccinations, or if a lack of passive antibody absorption is a possibility (i.e. inadequate nursing during the first few hours of life).

Those diseases which your puppy or adult dog should be routinely vaccinated against include distemper, parvovirus, infectious canine hepatitis (ICH), leptospirosis, canine cough (parainfluenza and bordetellosis), and rabies (see Table 4). The first five are normally administered as one injection; the bordetellosis vaccine is administered intranasally or by injection. In addition to the above-mentioned, a vaccine against Lyme disease is available, and should be administered to German Shorthaired Pointers that hunt in areas infested with ticks that carry the disease.

Canine Distemper

This infamous viral disease of dogs used to be one of the leading causes in death in unvaccinated puppies throughout the world. Although the incidence of this disease has decreased dramatically over the years due to vaccination programs, the distemper virus is still out there and can strike without warning. Infected dogs shed the disease in all body excretions, and transmission usually occurs via airborne means. As a result, like canine cough, it is highly contagious and can travel some distance on an air current. Distemper is considered a multifaceted disease; that is, it can affect a number of different body systems, including the respiratory, gastrointestinal, and nervous systems. Coughing, breathing difficulties, eye and nose discharges, vomiting and diarrhea, blindness, paralysis, and seizures are just some of the clinical signs that can result from infection. In those dogs that do not die from the disease, serious side effects from the

Parvovirus can be devastating to the unvaccinated pup.

disease can plague them the rest of their lives. Unfortunately, as with other viral diseases, there is no specific treatment once a dog becomes infected.

Parvovirus

First identified in 1977, this virus commonly strikes young, unvaccinated puppies under the age of six weeks, although all ages can be susceptible to infection. It is highly contagious, spreading from dog to dog via oral contamination with infected feces. Parvovirus affects the intestines, causing severe diarrhea and dehydration. In addition, the disease causes immune system depression, leaving the infected dog wide open to infection by other opportunistic organisms. In some puppies, the heart can be affected by the virus, leading to sudden death due to heart failure.

Infectious Canine Hepatitis (ICH)

This disease is found worldwide and is readily transmissible from dog to dog via contact with all types of body excretions, especially the urine. As the name implies, once the organism enters the dog's body, it causes a severe inflam-

mation of the liver, or hepatitis. However, ICH does not stop there. Other organ systems, including the eyes and kidneys, are often attacked as well. Clinical signs of this disease include abdominal pain, jaundice, and internal bleeding. A characteristic lesion of infectious canine hepatitis is called "blue eye." In this condition, one or both eyes can take on a blue appearance due to fluid buildup and inflammation within the eye(s).

Leptospirosis

Canine leptospirosis is a bacterial disease of dogs characterized by jaundice, vomiting, and kidney failure. At least four different groups of leptospirosis organisms, all belonging to the genus and species *Leptospira interrogans*, have been implicated in this disease in dogs. Remarkably enough, most infections are subclinical; that is, few show clinical signs of disease. When clinical signs do arise, however, the results can be serious, even life-threatening. Liver, kidney, and blood involvement can lead to intense vomiting and diarrhea, along with anemia and internal bleeding.

Dogs become infected with the organisms through contact with infected urine. Leptospirosis is more likely to show up in kennels where dogs are kept together under poor sanitary conditions. However, Shorthairs hunting on land occupied by feral dogs, coyotes, and/or wolves, and drinking from stagnant water pools on such land, are at risk as well.

Kennel Cough (Parainfluenza and Bordetellosis)

In the past, many pet owners regarded this respiratory disease as unimportant unless their pets were to be boarded or kept in a kennel environment (hence the disease's nickname). True, it occurs more frequently in such surroundings, and in other areas where dogs may be congregated (i.e. grooming salons, dog shows, etc.), but it is by no means restricted to these. The disease is highly contagious, transmitted by air and wind currents contaminated with cough and sneeze droplets from infected dogs. For this reason, all dogs, young and old, kenneled and unkenneled, can be threatened. The classical clinical sign associated with an uncomplicated case of canine cough is a relentless dry, hacking cough.

There is no one organism on which to solely place the blame for this disease; in fact, more than six different causative agents have been isolated, causing disease by themselves or in combination with the others. The two most important of these agents include a bacterium called *Bordetella bronchiseptica* and the canine parainfluenza virus. The former is related to the bacterium that causes whooping cough in humans. It results in the most severe form of the affliction, and can cause permanent damage to the airways if not treated soon enough.

Rabies

If there was ever a disease to strike fear into the hearts and minds of pet owners everywhere, this is it! Rabies is a deadly viral disease that can infect any warm-blooded mammal. The incidence of rabies within the United States varies with each state, depending upon the normal fauna found in that state, and on existing vaccination laws.

The rabies virus is most commonly transmitted via the saliva of infected animals, usually through a bite wound or contamination of existing open wounds or exposed mucous membranes. The disease is uniformly fatal once contracted.

Studies have shown that rabies occurs in higher incidence in younger dogs, the median age being about one year. In addition, due to hormonally

Interaction with skunks and other wild animals in the field can put your hunting dog at risk of exposure to rabies.

related roaming and territorial instincts, male dogs are at greater risk of exposure than are females. Traditionally, when we speak of rabies, a picture of a snarling, frothing, dog snapping at anything in sight comes to mind. In reality though, rabies may also show up as a mere behavioral change accompanied by a progressive incoordination and paralysis. As a result, rabies should be suspected anytime a dog exhibits behavioral changes accompanied by unexplained symptoms involving the nervous system. Unfortunately, the only way to definitively diagnose a case of rabies is to have a laboratory analysis performed on the animal's brain tissue, which means, of course, euthanasia of the animal in question.

Lyme Disease

In recent years, Lyme disease has come to the forefront in public awareness due to its ability to cause human illness. The disease, caused by the bacterium *Borrelia burgdorferi*, is primarily spread to dogs and to humans through the bite of an infected tick. For more information on Lyme disease, see page 54.

HOW-TO:
Giving Your German Shorthaired Pointer a Physical Examination

The next time your Shorthair goes in for an exam, ask your veterinarian to explain each step of the process so that you will be able to perform cursory exams at home.

Begin at your dog's head and work backwards toward the tail, checking each body part for abnormalities as you go.

Eyes: Redness, cloudiness, discharge (or drainage), squinting or unequal pupil sizes may signify trouble. In hunters, it could signify the presence of a foreign body in the eye. Such signs can also be caused by infection, trauma, and glaucoma. The whites of the eyes (called scleras) should be just that—white. If inflammation is present, the scleras are usually reddened. Yellow-tinged scleras (jaundice) may indicate the presence of a serious condition, such as liver failure. A thorough exam by a veterinarian is the only way to determine the cause of the jaundice.

Check the eyelids. Be sure that no foreign objects, eyelashes, or hairs are irritating the surfaces of the eyes. Constant, untreated irritation can lead to corneal injuries, which are extremely painful. German Shorthaired Pointers can be predisposed to a genetic disorder of the third eyelid or nictitating membrane, the white surface structure located on the inner corners of the eyes. This malady, called eversion of the nictitating membrane, is characterized by an outward "rolling" or folding of this structure, leading to the entrapment of dirt and debris, and subsequent eye irritation. Another condition that can involve the third eyelid involves the prolapse of the gland of the third eyelid, commonly known as cherry eye. This condition is identified as a prominent red swelling or bulge protruding from the third eyelid of one or both eyes. Cherry eye can also lead to secondary irritation caused by the entrapment of foreign matter on the eye surface.

Ears: Inspect the ears of your companion and note any foul smell or discharge. A black or brown discharge could signify an ear mite infestation or a yeast infection. A yellowish, creamy discharge means a bacterial infection or foreign body is present. Other signs of ear disease include constant scratching at the ears, head shaking, and the presence of a head tilt.

Nose: Discharges from the nostrils should always alert you to a potential disease challenge. Clear nasal discharges are caused by either allergies or viral infections. A green, mucoid discharge indicates bacterial infection, which can often occur secondarily to a foreign object lodged within the nose. Blood coming from the nose can result from trauma, tumors, foreign bodies, or blood-clotting disorders. Visually observe for tumors and ulcerations affecting the mucous membranes of the nose.

Mouth: Gently open your dog's mouth by grasping the head and upper jaw with one hand, tilting the head back and using your other hand to separate the jaws. The gums and mucous membranes within the mouth should be moist and pink. Pale, dry mucous membranes may indicate anemia, dehydration, or shock. If you suspect a problem, you should check the capillary refill time. Press on the upper gum with your index finger. The gum region under your finger should turn white. Release the pressure and the gum should return to a pink color within two seconds. If it takes longer, consult your veterinarian. Further inspect the mouth for swollen gums, foreign objects, tumors, ulcerations, and sores. A foul odor exuding from the mouth can be caused by excessive dental tartar or it could be caused by tumors or infections in the mouth itself.

Body: Run your hands over your bird dog's entire body and feel for any lumps or bumps. If you think you feel an abnormal mass, compare it to the other side. If you have any doubt that what you feel is normal, you should consult your veterinarian. Lumps can be abscesses, enlarged lymph nodes, cysts, foreign bodies, soft tissue swellings (such as hernias and bruises), or cancer. The earlier you detect and treat cancer, the better the chances are for complete recovery.

Be sure to check for lumps in the mammary region of female dogs (especially if they have not been spayed). The testicles of intact male dogs should be examined for abnormal swellings and masses. Intact male and female German Shorthaired Pointers run higher risks of developing cancer than neutered and spayed animals.

Look under the tail region for any lesions, masses, or discharges. Observe the region of the anal sacs. These sacs are located at the 4 o'clock and 8 o'clock positions beneath the dog's rectum. Normally, the dog will empty the sacs when it defecates. Occasionally, fluid may accumulate in the sacs, and they will need to be manually expressed.

Reproductive organs: Note any discharges coming from these areas. Not all discharges are abnormal, but some discharges indicate the presence of infections. For example, female dogs coming into heat may have a normal bloody discharge lasting up to three weeks. In addition, male dogs may normally have a small amount of green, mucuslike discharge around the opening of their prepuce. Often a fetid odor is the first noticeable sign of a problem discharge. In addition, affected dogs often act sick and may run fevers. Obviously, if you have any doubt whether or not a discharge is normal, consult your veterinarian.

The abdomen: The stomach, intestines, liver, pancreas, spleen, and kidneys are all located within the abdomen. Gently press both sides of the abdomen just behind the ribcage (some dogs may immediately become tense when you do this). Slowly work your way to the hip region, gently pressing as you go. Unless you have training in palpation, don't expect to know what you are feeling. The purpose of this exercise is to detect any swelling, tenderness, pain, or obvious masses involving the abdomen. If you feel anything strange, seek the opinion of your veterinarian.

Skin and coat: Evaluate your Pointer's skin and coat carefully. Signs of skin problems include hair loss, itchiness, redness, oiliness, scaliness, crustiness, and infection. Look closely for parasites, such as fleas and ticks, which can wreak havoc on a dog's integument. Poor nutrition and metabolic disorders (such as hypothyroidism) can cause a dog's hair to become dull and lifeless.

Legs: Run your hands down each of your dog's legs, noting any swelling or painful areas. Lymphedema is an inherited condition that can afflict German Shorthaired Pointer puppies, and, if the puppy survives, carries over into adulthood. This condition causes swelling in the extremities of affected individuals, and can become quite painful if secondary inflammation results (see Lymphedema, page 46). Check the pressure points over the elbows, knees, and wrists for signs of hair loss and/or irritation. Pressure point granulomas are not uncommon in German Shorthaired Pointers housed on hard surfaces. Finally, check the length of the nails. With your dog's paws planted squarely on the floor, the nails should barely touch the floor surface, if at all. If contact is noticeable, a nail trim is in order.

Report any abnormal findings discovered during your examination to your veterinarian as soon as possible. The quicker any condition is treated, the better the chances for a complete, uncomplicated recovery.

Internal Parasite Control

To ensure that your gun dog remains free of intestinal parasites such as roundworms, hookworms, and whipworms, stool checks should be performed yearly by your veterinarian. Early detection and treatment of worm infestations will help prevent malnutrition, diarrhea, and stress-related immune suppression from becoming established and complicating any pre-existing medical conditions. It will also lessen the risk of human exposure to these parasites, many of which can pose a significant health risk to people, especially children.

Environmental management and cleanliness also play a key role in the prevention of all internal parasites. Since fleas are the most common carrier of dog tapeworms, rigid flea control measures are essential to protect your dog against infestation by this type of worm. Furthermore, by disposing of, on a daily basis, any fecal material that may be deposited in your yard or near your pet's quarters by other dogs, transmission of infective parasite eggs will be effectively blocked.

If your dog is taking once-a-month heartworm preventive medication (if it isn't, it should be!), additional protection against intestinal worms may be afforded, depending upon the type being given. Check the label of the heartworm preventive medication you are using to see if it affords such protection against intestinal parasites. If not, consider asking your veterinarian to switch your dog over to one that does.

While on the subject of heartworms, *Dirofilaria immitis*, the canine heartworm, is one of the most devastating and life-threatening enemies of dogs, both young and old alike. Its presence within a dog's body can put an incredible burden on the heart, blood vessels, and other organs within the body, including the lungs, liver, and kidneys. In many cases, the concentration of these parasites becomes so great that affected dogs collapse and die suddenly without warning. Transmitted from dog to dog by mosquitoes, heartworms pose a risk wherever and whenever mosquitoes are found. Owing to the areas they commonly frequent while hunting, all gun dogs are especially at risk. Don't be fooled into thinking that just because your Shorthair may stay indoors most of the day that the threat is eliminated. Think about it: Have you ever seen a mosquito in your house? If you have, then your dog is at risk!

Although the disease caused by these internal parasites can be deadly, the good news is that canine heartworm disease is completely and easily preventable through the use of heartworm preventive medications. If your dog is not currently on a heartworm prevention program, call right now and schedule an appointment with your veterinarian to start one. As a responsible pet owner, you owe it to your hunting companion! In warmer climates where mosquitoes are present nearly year round, heartworm prevention needs to be given 12 months out of the year. In contrast, in those regions that experience seasonal changes and cooler temperatures, preventative measures need not be taken the entire year but only during the warmer mosquito season. Be sure to consult your veterinarian as to the proper preventative schedule to follow in your particular area.

Before starting a dog on heartworm preventive medication, a simple blood test needs to be performed to determine if exposure to heartworms has already occurred. If the test results are negative, then your dog may be started on a preventative. However, if the test returns positive for heartworms, preventive medication should not be started. Giving such medication to a dog already harboring adult heartworms and heartworm larvae circulating in the bloodstream could cause dangerous adverse reactions. Furthermore, if you are currently giving your pet preventive medication and you miss a scheduled treatment, always consult your veterinarian prior to resuming the treatments. Depending upon how late the treatment is, retesting may or may not be necessary. For those dogs on a seasonal prevention program, blood retesting should always be performed before the first preventative dose of medication of the season is given.

The most popular heartworm preventive medications come in tablet form, either chewable or nonchewable, and contain either ivermectin or milbemycin as the active ingredient. In the past, heartworm medication designed to be given daily was the only type of effective preventive medication available. Although the active ingredient of this daily preventive medicine, diethylcarbamazine, is also quite effective at preventing heartworms if administered consistently, it falls far short of the overall ease and efficacy of the newer preventatives. As a result, if you are currently giving your dog a daily pill, you should replace it with a once-a-month product.

External Parasite Control

Fleas are the most common external parasites that your German Shorthaired Pointer will have to contend with. Not only can their bites produce extreme discomfort and even allergic reactions, fleas are also host to the most common tapeworm that affects dogs, *Dipylidium caninum*.

To control fleas, you must treat not only your dog, but its environment as well. Your yard should be treated with insecticidal granules every six to eight weeks during the warm months of the year. For your house, consider using polymerized borate compounds, available under various brand names from your veterinarian or favorite pet supply. Sprinkled on the carpets and near the baseboards of your home, these compounds will kill all fleas that come in contact with them. Noticeable results are usually obtained within a week after application. Best of all, these powders are odorless, easy to use, and safe for pets and children. Under normal conditions, application of this product must be performed every six to twelve months. Carpets must remain dry for continued efficacy; if the carpet becomes damp or is shampooed, reapplication will be necessary.

For removing fleas on your dog, a number of options are available. Fipronil (Frontline®; Rhone Merieux, Inc.) kills adult fleas on dogs and helps to break the flea life cycle by killing immature fleas before they can lay eggs. This product is also effective against ticks that your German Shorthaired Pointer may encounter in the woods or field. Applied as a spray or topical drops, fipronil collects within the hair follicles and sebaceous glands of the skin, providing good residual action after initial application. Next, imidacloprid (Advantage®; Bayer Corporation) is another addition to the flea control arsenal that can be incorporated into a comprehensive flea control program. Imidacloprid works by killing adult fleas on contact, before they can lay eggs.

Fleas are the most common external parasites your dog will encounter.

Applied as topical drops on the back, the manufacturer of this product claims that it retains its effectiveness even after shampooing or repeated swimming. Finally, lufenuron (Program®; Ciba-Geigy Corporation) is a product designed to be taken internally by your dog. Available in tablet form, lufenuron exerts its flea control action by sterilizing the fleas that bite the dog, thereby rendering those fleas sterile. Since they cannot reproduce, fleas are eventually eliminated (in a contained environment) via attrition. It is important to remember that lufenuron does not actually kill fleas. As a result, products that kill adult fleas must be used in conjunction with this treatment in order to achieve effective flea control. As one might expect, many veterinarians recommend this product only for those dogs kept in an indoor (contained) environment.

Besides fleas, the next most prevalent external parasite that your German Shorthaired Pointer will likely encounter is the tick. Controlling ticks on your dog and in your environment is not only important for your pet's health, but for yours as well. These unsightly parasites, which attach themselves to their host via sucking mouthparts, can transmit serious diseases such as Rocky Mountain Spotted Fever and Lyme disease to pets and to people. As far as their canine hosts are concerned, untreated infestations can also lead to skin irritation and in severe cases, blood-loss anemia. Female ticks lay their eggs in and under sheltered areas in the environment, such as wood stumps, rocks, and wall crevices. Once hatched, the larvae, called "seed ticks," will crawl up onto grass stems or bushes and attach themselves to a host that may happen to pass by. Depending on their life cycle, immature ticks may seek out one to three different host animals to complete the maturation process into an adult.

Since ticks are sensitive to the same type of chemicals as are fleas, treatment and control is basically the same. Thorough and consistent treatment of the yard, and if needed, the house, with an approved insecticide is the cornerstone of an effective control program. Since ticks can live for months in their surrounding habitat without a blood meal, treatment should be performed every two to four weeks (as with fleas) during the peak flea and tick seasons in your area. A pyrethrin spray can be applied to your dog's haircoat prior to a trip to the field to discourage ticks from attaching. If a few happen to slip by, use the same pyrethrin spray to kill those that have attached to the skin. Never attempt to remove ticks from your dog by applying manual pressure alone, or by applying a hot match or needle to the tick's body. Most ticks first killed by the application of a pyrethrin spray will fall off with time once they die. In some cases, you may need to manually remove the dead tick after spraying. When picking them off your dog, never use your bare hands, in order to prevent accidental exposure to disease. Instead, use a pair of gloves and tweezers to grasp the dead tick as close to its attachment site as possible, then pull straight up using constant tension. Once the tick is freed, wash the bite wound with soap and water and then apply a first-aid cream or ointment to prevent infection. Again, be sure the tick is completely dead before removal; this will insure that the tick's mouthparts come out attached to the rest of the body. If left behind, the mouthparts can cause an irritating localized skin reaction.

Mange mites are microscopic parasites belonging to the same zoological class as spiders. They live within the skin or hair follicles of their host and feed on blood and cellular debris. Their presence often leads to intense itching, hair loss, and secondary skin infections in affected animals. The two most common types of mange affecting dogs are sarcoptic mange and demodectic mange. Diagnosis of mange can be made by your veterinarian by observing clinical signs and by examining skin scrapings obtained from your dog. Treatment for either type of mange employs the use of special dips designed to kill the mites. In addition, treatment for demodectic mange may also include the administration of antiparasitic drugs, and antibiotics if a secondary skin infection is present.

Grooming for Health

Grooming is an important part of any preventive health-care program. Not only will it help keep your dog in top shape physically, but the time spent with your friend will provide your Shorthair with the psychological comfort that such interaction and attention create. As an added benefit, routine grooming and hands-on attention will assist in the early detection of external parasites, tumors, infections, or any other changes or abnormalities that may result from the germination of an internal disease condition. Routine grooming for your German Short-haired Pointer should include skin and coat care (brushing, bathing), nail care, ear care, and dental care.

Brushing and Bathing

As a rule, if you brush your Shorthair on a daily basis, the need for bathing is minimal. Routine bathing should only be performed on those dogs that are continually exposed to excessive dirt, grease, or other noxious substances in their environment, and for those canines suffering from external parasites or medical conditions, such as infections and/or seborrhea of the skin.

If a general cleaning is desired for an otherwise healthy dog, then the best recommendation is to purchase

and use a mild hypoallergenic shampoo for this purpose. These shampoos are readily available from your veterinarian or favorite pet supply store. Remember, though, that if your dog is afflicted with any type of medical condition, then the type of shampoo used should be limited to that recommended or prescribed by your veterinarian.

Before giving your dog a bath, apply some type of protection to both eyes to prevent corneal burns if shampoo accidentally gets into the eyes. Mineral oil can be used for this purpose; however, a sterile ophthalmic ointment is preferred. Such an ointment can be purchased from your veterinarian or local pet store.

Nail Care

Your Pointer's nails should be examined every three to four weeks and trimmed at that time, if necessary. Overgrown, neglected nails will snag and tear easily, causing pain and discomfort. Additionally, nail overgrowth can lead to gait instability and joint

Nail trims are an integral part of any grooming program.

31

Daily brushing will keep your Shorthair's skin and coat healthy.

stress, two complications that your hunting dog does not need.

To determine whether or not your Pointer's nails are too long, observe the paws as they rest flat on the floor with your dog standing. If any nail touches the floor surface, it is a candidate for trimming. When trimming nails, use only a brand of nail clipper that is designed for dogs. If your dog's nails are clear, you should be able to note the line of demarcation between the pink quick (the portion of the nail that contains the blood supply) and the remaining portions of the nails. Using your pair of clippers, snip off the latter portion just in front of the quick. For those Shorthairs with darker nails, use a flashlight or penlight beam to illuminate the quick portion prior to trimming. If this still doesn't enable you to visualize the quick, trim off only small portions at a time until the nail is no longer bearing weight. If bleeding occurs, stop trimming and consider having your veterinarian finish the job. Although ideally you want to avoid

drawing blood when you are trimming your dog's nails, don't fret if you do so. Using a clean cloth or towel, simply apply direct pressure to the end of the bleeding nail for three to five minutes. In most cases, this is all that is needed to stop the bleeding. For stubborn cases, commercially available clotting powder can be applied to the end of the nail to help stop the hemorrhage.

Ear Care

Because the canine external ear canal is long, and because the ear flaps of German Shorthaired Pointers are pendulous, routine care for the ears is needed to prevent moisture, wax, and debris from accumulating. This involves cleaning and drying the ears on a bimonthly basis. Many different types of ear cleansers and drying agents are readily available from pet stores, pet supply houses, and veterinary offices. Liquid ear cleansers are preferred over powders, since powders tend to saturate with moisture and trap it within the ear canal. Most liquid ear cleansers contain both a wax solvent and drying agent (astringent) that clean the ear and dry it at the same time.

Before cleaning your dog's ears, take note of any signs of irritation, discharges, or foul odors. If one or all are noted, your pet's ears should be examined by your veterinarian in lieu of cleaning. This is recommended as well for Pointers that appear to be constantly shaking or tilting their heads. The reason for this is that unhealthy ears may have torn or diseased eardrums, and introducing a cleansing solution into such an ear can spread infection to the deeper portions and structures within the ear.

Assuming your dog's ears are healthy, begin cleaning by gently pulling the ear flap out and away from the head, exposing and straightening the ear canal. Carefully squeeze a liberal amount of ear-cleaning solution into the ear and massage the ear canal for twenty seconds. Next, allow your dog to shake its head, then proceed to the opposite ear and follow the same procedure. Once both ears have been treated, use cotton balls or swabs to remove any wax or debris found on the inside folds of the ear flap and the outer portions of the ear canal. To avoid serious injury to your dog's ear, never enter into the actual ear canal when swabbing.

Dental Care

Keeping your German Shorthaired Pointer's teeth free of tartar and plaque build-up is a preventive health care procedure that will in itself add years to the life of your four-legged friend. It is estimated that tooth and gum disease (periodontal disease) strikes more than 70 percent of all dogs by three years of age. Not only do plaque-laden teeth and inflamed gums lead to halitosis (foul breath) and eventual tooth loss, but bacteria from these sources can enter the bloodstream and travel to the heart and kidneys, where they can set up an infection. Infection of the heart valves and subsequent heart failure can all too often be traced back to periodontal disease. As a result, regular visits to your veterinarian for professional cleaning and polishing, supplemented by an at-home dental care program, are a must to keep your dogs teeth, and heart, healthy.

Because a short-acting sedative/anesthetic will be required for professional cleaning, blood tests should be performed on your dog prior to anesthesia to make certain that there are no underlying conditions which may complicate recovery. Once the dog is anesthetized, an ultrasonic scaler is used to shatter and break up the plaque that has accumulated on your dog's teeth above and below the gum-

Because the pendulous ear flaps of the Shorthair can predispose the ears to infection, good preventive care is a must.

line. After this has been completed, the mouth is rinsed and a polisher is used on the teeth to restore their smooth, shiny surfaces. The entire procedure should take no more than 30 to 40 minutes, after which time your pet will be recovered from the anesthesia.

Professional teeth cleaning such as that described above may be required every one to two years. However, with diligent dental care provided by you at home on a daily basis, this interval between treatments can be extended. Toothpastes and cleansing solutions designed for dogs are available from your veterinarian or local pet stores. For best results, use preparations that contain chlorhexidine, an antimicrobial agent that can provide hours of residual protection against bacteria that may attempt to colonize the tooth and gum surfaces. Do not use toothpastes designed for use in humans on your dog; these can cause severe stomach upset in your Shorthair if swallowed. A soft-bristled toothbrush or cloth should be used to gently massage the paste or solution onto the outer and, if possible, inner surfaces of the teeth and gums. If in doubt, don't hesitate to ask your veterinarian to demonstrate the safe and correct procedure for brushing canine teeth.

Special devices designed to help keep your dog's teeth free of tartar can also be used to supplement your efforts at home. Certain rawhide, nylon, and urethane chew bones are specially designed to massage and clean a dog's teeth while it is chewing on the device. In addition, flossing devices are commercially available that can help reduce tartar build-up more than with brushing alone. Ask your pet health professional for details on these and other methods for keeping your Pointer's teeth and gums disease-free.

Feeding Your German Shorthaired Pointer

There can be little doubt that proper nutrition is the cornerstone of an active, healthy life for your German Shorthaired Pointer. In addition, good nutritional management can have a profound positive impact on the performance in the field of this breed. Fortunately, as the amount of research supporting the link between diet and health increases each day, so does the quality of foods that are available for your pal to eat.

Hundreds of years ago, the diet of most domesticated dogs consisted primarily of table scraps, supplemented by whatever other consumables or prey they could uncover while roaming freely within the confines of their man-made territories. Today, the commercial dog food industry exceeds one hundred million dollars per year in the United States alone, with literally hundreds of products and brand names available for the choosing. As a result, your mission as a prudent dog owner is to choose the ration for your Short-

hair that is most nutritionally complete and balanced for its particular stage of life and activity level. Many breeders and trainers advocate the formulation of rations at home using meat and other natural ingredients as raw materials. While such rations can provide excellent nutrition, it is vital that they be prepared properly and contain a balance of nutrients that can be readily absorbed by the dog. Dog food companies invest millions of dollars in research into their premium foods, ensuring that they are of superior nutritional quality. The bottom line: Unless you simply enjoy putting in the time and effort preparing your friend's meal, feeding a homemade ration affords no advantages over feeding a high-quality, premium commercial diet.

Nutritional Guidelines for Puppies

For German Shorthaired Pointers, puppyhood begins at birth and lasts for approximately 14 months. During this stage of life, your puppy will need to take in appropriate levels of calcium and phosphorus, protein, vitamins, and energy (calories) to ensure proper growth. To be sure your puppy receives the nutrition it needs for correct development, it should be fed a high-quality, nutritionally balanced premium puppy food. Shop for quality, not price, when selecting a food for your pup. Since there are so many to choose from commercially, ask your veterinarian which one he/she recommends. Remember that the first year of your puppy's life sets the stage for the degree of health and happiness in later years. As a result, investing in good nutrition during this crucial stage of life is vital.

When feeding high-quality, premium diets to your puppy, vitamin and mineral supplementation is generally not required. Feed the manufacturer's recommended daily amount for the size and weight of your little one. Divide the daily allowance into two feedings, the first to be offered in the morning and the second in the evening. Leave the food down for 20 minutes, allowing your pup to eat all it wishes in that time, and then remove the food entirely until the next meal. Your puppy will quickly learn to eat on schedule if it expects to fulfill its appetite.

Obviously, avoid giving table food, table "scraps," or treats and snacks to your puppy, as this will surely upset the balance of its daily nutrition. As you know, puppies (especially hungry ones) love to explore their environment with their mouths, or more specifically, with their teeth! As a result, keep plenty of nylon chew bones lying about with which your pup can satisfy its urge to chew between meals.

Keep plenty of clean, fresh water accessible at all times for your young hunter. Filtered water is recommended for canines for the same reasons it is recommended for humans. Be sure to change the water daily and thoroughly clean the water bowl at least once per week.

Nutritional Guidelines for Mature Dogs

At 12 months of age, plan on switching your bird dog over to a maintenance-type diet for adults. If possible, use the same brand of food (same manufacturer) to ensure the transition to the adult ration is smooth. Be aware that so-called maintenance foods that make the claim "complete and balanced for all life stages" are actually puppy foods, since they have been formulated to meet the needs of the most demanding life stage, growth. As a result, they contain an excess of nutrients for the adult dog. Just as researchers have found that the excessive intake of certain dietary nutrients (like phosphorus, sodium, and fat) is harmful for humans over long periods, certain excesses may

also contribute to diseases like kidney failure, heart failure, obesity, and diabetes in dogs as they grow older. Also, we know that reducing the level of key nutrients in the adult's diet to meet but not greatly exceed its needs is never harmful. Good quality, scientifically designed, adult-maintenance diets always contain these reduced and balanced nutrient levels, and are the rations of choice.

Most adult dogs can be fed just once a day. As far as amounts are concerned, use the manufacturer's recommended daily feeding amounts, then make some adjustments according to your dog's individual needs and activity levels. For instance, daily caloric needs will generally need to be increased 35 to 40 percent during field training and during hunting season as compared to other times of the year. Also, some dogs will gain weight as they grow older despite eating a recommended daily amount of an adult maintenance diet. Further reducing the portion size for these pets usually results in an unhappy, hungry dog that whines, begs, raids garbage, and otherwise protests the unpleasant side effects of a diet. Instead, if you find that your four-legged friend has put on a few extra pounds along its midsection, it should be placed on a medically supervised weight-loss program, consisting of increased exercise and a reduced-calorie ration, which is designed to satisfy your pet's hunger without the calories.

As far as treats for your German Shorthaired Pointer are concerned, they are best reserved for training sessions. However, understanding that even the strongest of willpowers can be shattered in an instance by a pair of forlorn, begging eyes, feel free to keep some kibbles of your dog's regular food handy and offer them as treats between full meals. Or, strange as it may sound, fresh vegetables cut

Keep food and water bowls clean and easily accessible.

As with puppies, fresh water (preferably filtered) should be made available at all times for your adult bird dog. Be sure to change its water daily and thoroughly clean the water bowl at least once per week.

Nutrition for Senior Adults

Once your German Shorthaired Pointer reaches seven years of age, dietary changes are warranted to accommodate the effects of aging and the wear and tear on the organ systems of its body. The goal of this senior nutritional program is to provide the highest level of nutrition possible, while at the same time maintaining an ideal body weight, slowing the progression of disease and age-related changes, and reducing or eliminating the clinical manifestations of specific disease conditions. For instance, as your dog's metabolic rate slows and the tendency toward obesity increases with advancing age, increasing the amount of fiber and reducing the amount of fat in the diet can help keep the caloric intake where it needs to be to keep body weight constant. In addition, as the kidneys begin to lose their ability to handle the waste materials that must be removed from body, dietary adjustments can play a major role in reducing the amount of waste products the kidneys have to process. Simply reducing the sodium content of a ration can have a significant effect of reducing the workload placed on an aging heart. Finally, since older pets tend to have reduced sensory output (taste and smell), increasing the palatability of a diet can keep even the most finicky senior satisfied. This can be accomplished by warming the food prior to feeding, mixing a small amount of warm water in with the dry ration, or by adding flavor enhancers recommended by your veterinarian. Older dogs suffering from diseased teeth and gums will often go off their

into bite-size pieces make excellent, low-calorie treats as well. You'll be surprised how many dogs just love vegetables to munch on. Remember: Dogs naturally don't need dietary variations to satisfy cravings. However, they can learn to crave certain items and become finicky eaters if constantly offered items other than those mentioned.

Do not offer bones of any kind to your German Shorthaired Pointer, as they can shatter, splinter, or become lodged in the mouth, throat, and gastrointestinal tract. Bones can also lead to nutritional imbalances by adding unwanted amount of minerals to the diet. Even rawhide bones can pose a threat to an overzealous Pointer that doesn't like to chew its food, as large pieces of slowly digested rawhide can cause gastrointestinal upset and, in severe instances, intestinal blockages. Instead, stick with flavored nylon chew bones. These are available at any pet store and work great as substitutes for real bones and rawhide. Most importantly, nylon bones are easily digested if consumed, even in large chunks.

feed due to the pain associated with chewing. Also, dogs that are experiencing a diminished sense of smell due to some type of nasal impediment can also become picky eaters. Needless to say, if you ever notice your dog's food intake decrease over a week, contact your pet's doctor. A check-up may be in order just to be on the safe side to be sure the loss of appetite is not the result of a serious underlying medical disorder.

For healthy, older dogs, a high-quality ration formulated for "senior" or "older" dogs is indicated. These foods typically contain more fiber and less fat to accommodate a slowing metabolism associated with age. Increases in fiber content also serve to promote healthy bowel function in older pets. Again, stick with the same brand of food you have been feeding over the years to help prevent digestive upset when the transition occurs.

If your German Shorthaired Pointer is suffering from a specific illness, a special diet available from your veterinarian is required. For example, dogs suffering from constipation, certain types of colitis, and diabetes mellitus often require a fiber content in their ration even greater than that found in standard "senior" formulas. In addition, those older dogs suffering from chronic diarrhea, excessive gas production, and/or pancreatic problems can often benefit from special diets formulated to be more easily digestible than standard maintenance rations. Recommended dietary management of dogs suffering from heart and/or kidney disease includes diets low in sodium and restricted in protein. Remember, because all of these prescribed diets are so specialized, be sure to follow your veterinarian's directions closely as to the amount and frequency of feedings.

Be sure both food and water bowls are easily accessible to older dogs. Poor eyesight and/or arthritic joints can sometimes make it difficult to reach or find the water bowl. Keep fresh, clean water available at all times. Keep in mind that dogs suffering from kidney impairment or endocrine diseases such as diabetes may drink (and require) excessive amounts of water, requiring you to refill the water dish several times per day.

Weight Control

Keeping your hunting dog's weight under control is one the most effective ways to add years to its life and to improve its effectiveness in the field. Obesity can be defined as an increase in body fat resulting in an increase in body weight more than ten percent the normal weight standard for the dog's breed or body type. This standard for German Shorthaired Pointers is 55 pounds for smaller males; 70 pounds for larger ones. Female German Shorthaired Pointers should range in weight between 45 and 60 pounds, depending upon body type. Your veterinarian can help determine your dog's body type, and hence, its ideal weight.

Senior adults have different nutritional requirements than their younger counterparts.

Indiscriminate feeding practices can lead to obesity.

Obesity is undoubtedly one of the most prevalent diseases affecting dogs today. Overweight dogs are pre-disposed to a variety of other serious disorders such as hypertension, car-diac fatigue, pancreatitis, diabetes mellitus, and colitis. Skin disorders seem to be more prevalent in over-weight dogs, as do disorders of the musculoskeletal system and nervous system, including intervertebral disc disease and, in hunters like the Shorthair, osteoarthrosis and arthritis. Obviously, the stamina and speed of a bird dog will be adversely affected if it is carrying around excess bag-gage, not to mention that the chances of injury occurring in the field are greatly increased.

There is no doubt that the primary cause of obesity in dogs is dietary indiscretion; that is, feeding food items other than the dog's normal food.

Included in such foods are table scraps, a favorite target of most ambi-tious canines. Tempted by big, sad eyes, owners who succumb to such emotion do nothing but promote weight gain and create an annoying beggar out of their once-disciplined comrade. Failure to eliminate bad habits such as this will lead to unprecedented weight gain, especially as your dog matures and its overall metabolism slows.

If your Shorthair is "unfashionably heavy," simply cutting back on the amount you feed will not provide the lasting weight loss you desire. In fact, depriving your dog of adequate amounts of food could create a state of malnutrition, leading to incessant begging and dietary indiscretions. The correct way to achieve weight loss through dietary adjustment is to feed your dog a ration that is specially for-mulated for weight loss. These diets are readily available from your veteri-narian and should be fed under your clinician's direction. They generally contain a high-fiber content, which allows for calorie reduction while satis-fying the hunger of your pet. Feed the amount recommended on the bag or can that corresponds to your pet's ideal weight. If you don't know what this should be, your veterinarian can assist you in making that determina-tion. In addition, to provide added sat-isfaction for your dog, divide the total daily ration into three or four feedings over the course of a day.

Nutrition During Training and Hunting Season

German Shorthaired Pointers that are being trained in the field or for ring hunt require extra nutrition to counter-act the additional energy expenditures needed for these activities. As a rule, working dogs will require a caloric increase of 35 to 40 percent over the amount required of the more sedentary canine. These dogs will need to extract more energy from their diet; as a result, foods fed for this purpose must be nutritionally dense and highly digestible. Foods with high-energy density contain higher amounts of fat, which provides more calories per gram than do proteins or carbohydrates. Highly digestible foods refer to those rations that can be consumed in smaller amounts (compared to foods that are less digestible), while still meeting the dog's energy needs. Whenever feeding a highly dense and digestible diet, be sure your dog has access to plenty of water at all times. One big advantage of feeding such a diet is that your dog doesn't have to eat as much as it would in order to receive adequate nutritional energy. As a result, chances are, when it begins its work, there won't be any food in the stomach to slow it down. Dogs fed these rations do not have to defecate as often, eliminating another distraction to the hunter in the field.

During hunting season, feed your bird dog twice a day, feeding 25 percent of the ration two hours prior to the activity, and the remainder of the diet one hour following its cessation. Never feed your dog within one hour of rigorous physical activity, as doing so could predispose it to stomach bloat, a dangerous medical condition.

Once hunting season is over, switch back to your dog's off-season diet and feeding frequency. Remember, if activity level does not justify added caloric intake, undesirable weight gain will result.

Exercising Your German Shorthaired Pointer

Implementing a moderate exercise program into the daily routine of your German Shorthaired Pointer will reap multiple health benefits for your four-legged friend. It will improve the dog's cardiovascular endurance and function,

German Shorthaired Pointers can make great jogging companions.

allowing it to go for long distances for long periods of time which can prove to be a great benefit on a busy all-day hunt. In addition, physical exercise helps tone and tighten the muscles and improve recovery times, allowing your dog to go longer and harder during the hunt. For Shorthairs not used for hunting, it will help maintain muscle tone and strength in otherwise sedentary dogs. Exercise will also improve your hunter's agility and flexibility, and help loosen up any stiff joints. Regular exercise will also promote and improve gastrointestinal motility, stimulating nutrient absorption and ensuring maximum utilization. Finally, keeping your dog physically fit will help keep its weight in check, preventing obesity and all of the health ramifications that come with it.

Before implementing any exercise program for your German Shorthaired Pointer, a complete physical exam should be performed by your veterinarian to identify any underlying health conditions that may limit the type and amount of exercise performed. Be sure to follow your veterinarian's advice closely in designing a fitness program around the special needs of your individual pet.

There are several avenues to take in order to heighten and strengthen your Shorthair's cardiovascular endurance and muscle fitness. Swimming is a great exercise and can often be combined with retrieval training. It is especially useful for increasing cardiovascular endurance and toning particular muscle groups. Another conditioning method used by a number of trainers is to bike with their dog alongside them down country roads at a speed that allows the dog to maintain a brisk walk or slow trot. If this method is used, distance needs to be increased slightly during each week of training. As a rule of thumb, begin the first week at one mile per session, increasing it the following week to one and a half miles, then two miles the next week, increasing it a half of a mile each week thereafter until your dog can go comfortably three and a half to four and a half miles

Be sure your dog is well-conditioned when hunting season arrives.

without becoming overly winded or tired. As an alternative, you may want to take up a jogging program with your dog. Owing to the size of German Shorthaired Pointers, they make great jogging partners and can keep up with the greatest foot racers. However, check with your doctor before undertaking such a program yourself!

Be sure to allow a ten-minute warm-down following any strenuous activity. Also, provide your Pointer access to plenty of fresh water to allow for replacement of fluids lost due to physical exertion. Isotonic sport drinks or electrolyte formulas available from your local convenience store or grocery are also effective means of replenishing lost fluids and electrolytes.

Physical Conditioning for Hunting Season

About 60 days prior to the beginning of hunting season you should plan on implementing a conditioning program for both you and your dog in order to prepare you physically for the big days that lie ahead. As far as your dog's conditioning program is concerned, plan on gradually increasing the number of trips into the field as time permits. Ideally, if you can get into the field three to five times weekly, 45 to 90 minutes at a time, your dog will undoubtedly be in top condition when hunting season arrives. Beginning a conditioning program early will also allow time for your dog's foot pads to toughen and to prepare for the rough fields and woods it is likely to encounter in the days to come.

Neutering for Health

The term neutering refers to the removal of the ovaries and uterus (ovariohysterectomy) in the female dog or the testicles (castration) in the male. Because of the high incidence of reproductive disorders in older dogs, it is recommended that all dogs be neutered by their eighth birthday. By having this procedure performed, age-related uterine infections and pyometra in older females can be avoided, and the incidence of prostate disorders in aging males greatly reduced. As an added benefit, if you are not planning on breeding your female, those dogs that have had this procedure performed prior to their second heat cycle have a lesser risk of developing mammary cancer at a later age than are their non-neutered counterparts.

Following the administration of anesthesia, the actual procedure should take no more than twenty-five minutes to perform. Following post-operative recovery, a physical examination will once again be performed prior to your pet being sent home. Sutures are normally removed seven to ten days following the surgery.

Contrary to popular belief, neutering your dog won't lead to laziness and obesity. There are plenty of examples of slim and trim neutered dogs running around debunking this myth! Improper feeding practices, lack of exercise, and, in some instances, disease, cause obesity in dogs, not reproductive status. Furthermore, while it is true that neutering can have a calming effect on nervous or restless Shorthairs, activity levels in emotionally stable dogs are rarely affected.

Traveling with Your Shorthair

In all instances involving transport of a dog by car, the safety and comfort of the passenger (and driver, when applicable) must always be kept in mind first and foremost. You as a responsible pet owner can help achieve these goals by following a few basic travel guidelines.

To begin, it is always recommended that, when transporting a pet by automobile, a travel carrier or kennel be used. Not only will your pet feel more secure in a carrier, helping to reduce

Your dog's travel kennel should be large enough for it to turn around in, yet small enough to prevent unnecessary movement during transport.

stress associated with the ride, but it will help minimize jostling and jolting movements that could injure your dog. If your Pointer is too large to fit comfortably into one of these carriers, then the back seat is the place to be, not the front seat! An excited or stressed-out, unrestrained pet in the passenger seat of an automobile creates a very dangerous driving condition. In addition, dogs allowed to ride in front seats can suffer serious or even lethal injuries should airbags deploy in an accident.

Be sure to keep the inside of your car well-ventilated and at a cool temperature. Excited or stressed canines forced to travel in hot, stuffy car interiors, or ones filled with cigarette or cigar smoke, are likely to suffer ill effects. Cigarette smoke in itself can be quite irritating to the eyes, nose, and mucous membranes of your dog. As a result, as a courtesy to your canine friend, refrain from smoking until you have reached your final destination. Car exhaust fumes can have the same effect as cigarette smoke. As a result, if stopped in traffic for any appreciable amount of time, be sure to open the car windows

41

Whenever possible, confine your Shorthair to a carrier or crate when traveling by car or truck.

slightly and keep the air within the car circulating continuously.

As you have heard time and time again, never leave your dog in a parked car unattended for more than five minutes on days when temperatures exceed 72°F (22°C) or drop below 55°F (13°C), because heat stroke or hypothermia (respectively) could result. If you do have to leave your pet for a few minutes, be sure to leave two or more windows partially opened to allow for air circulation. In addition, the use of window shields and sun visors is strongly recommended to help keep the temperature within the car at an acceptable level.

For lengthy trips, be sure to take along plenty of water for your dog to drink. Additionally, plan on making frequent "potty" stops along the way. Here is a useful tip: Consider freezing some water in a bowl prior to the trip. This "popsicle" can provide a lasting and refreshing source of water for extended travel.

If your dog has a tendency toward motion sickness, try feeding a small amount of food about 30 minutes prior to your trip. Often, an empty stomach coupled with stress can predispose a pet to motion sickness. Never give your dog any medication for anxiety or motion sickness unless it was specifically prescribed by your veterinarian.

When transporting your German Shorthaired Pointer by airplane, precautions should be taken. Always consult your veterinarian beforehand to determine whether or not any medical conditions your pet may have could be exacerbated by such a trip. For example, high-altitude flying and potential temperature/pressure fluctuations could prove to be harmful to a dog that may be suffering from an underlying heart disorder. Speak with an airline representative concerning their accommodations for traveling pets. Variations in policies do exist between airline companies; again, don't hesitate to ask your pet health professionals for their recommendations.

Selected Diseases and Conditions in German Shorthaired Pointers

When it comes to health, German Shorthaired Pointers (as with all dogs) are just like humans. Some will go through their entire lives without any health problems along the way; others just seem to be prone to every illness that comes along. A number of factors play a role in the susceptibility of your German Shorthaired Pointer to illness, including genetics, environment, nutrition, immune system strength, and, very importantly, the extent of preventive health care provided to it by you. In fact, for a dog that may be genetically prone to illness or injury, preventive health care can do wonders to help counteract some of these inherent defects. Unfortunately, many dog owners fail to realize the importance of preventive health care; as a result, their four-legged companion may ultimately pay the price later on.

German Shorthaired Pointers are not unique in their predisposition and susceptibility to common canine diseases, disorders, and injuries. Like other breeds, they can suffer their fair share of viral diseases like parvovirus and distemper, organ dysfunctions like kidney failure and heart disease, parasitic infestations, including intestinal worms and heartworm disease, and injuries involving the bones, tendons, and muscles. As a result, it is beyond the scope of this book to provide a comprehensive review of all of the

potential health challenges that your German Shorthaired Pointer may face. There are numerous excellent books

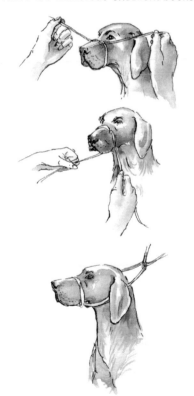

Ill or injured dogs may bite due to fear or pain; as a result, don't hesitate to apply a muzzle as necessary unless the dog is vomiting or having difficulty breathing.

on the market today that focus specifically on diseases and disorders in dogs. Ask your veterinarian to recommend one and purchase it.

Health disorders of dogs can be placed into eight categories, depending upon the underlying origin of the disorder. Understand that there can be a variety of overlap between these categories, with one predisposing to the formation of another, or two or more categories existing together.

Traumatic/Toxic Disorders

Traumatic disorders include not only those produced by direct, external physical trauma (i.e. fracture), but also those produced by trauma occurring to an organ or organ system from within. Examples of items that can cause damage from within include poisons and foreign bodies. German Shorthaired Pointers used for hunting will

Performing CPR.

undoubtedly earn their fair share of sprains, bruises, and sore muscles. Snakebite, poisoned predator baits, and accidental gunshot are additional risks that a hunting dog could be exposed to in the field.

If you do encounter a sudden injury or illness affecting your German Shorthaired Pointer either at home or in the field, don't panic! This will only hinder your first-aid efforts. The ultimate goal of any first aid is simple: To stabilize your dog's condition until professional medical care can be obtained. Certainly the first item that needs to be determined is whether or not a life-threatening situation exists. Cessation of breathing or heartbeat, severe bleeding, and poisoning all demand immediate attention. Once these situations have been addressed, you can then direct your attention toward other less serious challenges.

In the event of a sudden injury or illness, it may become necessary to perform cardiopulmonary resuscitation.

The combination of artificial respiration and external heart massage is termed cardiopulmonary resuscitation (CPR). Artificial respiration is indicated if your dog has stopped breathing. In addition, if the heart has stopped beating, external heart massage must be instituted in conjunction with the artificial respiration (Note: Never apply heart massage if the heart is still beating. To do so could actually lead to heart failure). The purpose of CPR is to supply oxygen to the lungs and to keep the blood circulating until your dog can resume these functions itself.

To perform artificial respiration for the dog that has stopped breathing, first use your finger to clear the mouth of any blood, mucus, vomit, or other debris that may be present. Tilt the head back to straighten the airway, then clasp the mouth shut with your hand and place your mouth over your dog's nose and mouth, forming a tight seal. Blow into the nose until you see the chest expand. (If a small puppy is involved, deliver gentle puffs of breath to prevent overinflation of the lungs.) If you don't see the chest expand, repeat the first two steps, then try again. If there is still no expansion, probe the back of the throat for a foreign body obstructing the airway. Release the seal, allowing your pet to fully exhale. Repeat this sequence once every five seconds until normal breathing resumes or until veterinary assistance is obtained.

To perform CPR on a dog whose heart has stopped, first perform artificial respiration, then lay the dog on its right side and place the heel of one hand on the rib cage just behind the elbow. Place your other hand on top of the first. Firmly and smoothly, compress the chest three to four inches using both hands. Each compression should last approximately one-half second.

Perform these chest compressions at a rate of one per second. After every ten compressions, perform an artificial respiration. Check for a heartbeat after every second cycle.

Continue this sequence until the heartbeat resumes or until veterinary care is obtained.

Inherited Diseases

Inherited diseases may be considered birth defects; however, many do not become apparent until a dog is several months old. If you are selecting a German Shorthaired Pointer for the first time, or if you are planning on building a small (or large) business around a German Shorthaired Pointer breeding program, there are several inherited (genetic) disorders that can show up in this breed of which you should be aware. Genetic defects are not especially common, yet when they do rear their ugly head, they can be quite devastating to the individual and to a breeding program.

Several factors will influence the health of your German Shorthaired Pointer, including genetics, environment, nutrition, immune system integrity, and preventive care provided.

Genetic disorders show up as abnormalities in either the anatomy or cellular/organ function of affected dogs. Clinical signs associated with the defect will vary, depending upon the type and severity of the disorder, and may affect more than just one of the dog's body systems at the same time.

Genetically based diseases can be controlled by neutering known defective or carrier animals. Such animals sometimes may be difficult to identify if the defect is not outwardly noticeable. However, ethical and prudent breeders, when suspicious that a "bad" gene may be lurking within their breeding stock, will do everything in their power to purge this gene from their midst, even going so far as to perform "test" matings in order to identify potential carriers. Obviously, this is the type of breeder you will want to deal with when purchasing your German Shorthaired Pointer.

When buying a German Shorthaired Pointer, there are a number of steps or precautions you should take to reduce the chances of unknowingly purchasing a dog with a genetic defect or one harboring a defective gene. To begin, only deal with reputable breeders when selecting your German Shorthaired Pointer. Always ask for references of owners who have purchased puppies originating from the breeding pair your puppy will come from, and call them all! Next, always examine your puppy's pedigree prior to purchase. Discuss any questions you may have with the breeder and be sure you feel comfortable with the answers you get. Finally, be sure to give your puppy a thorough checkover in its own environment, and insist on a veterinary physical exam by a veterinarian of your choice.

The German Shorthaired Pointer breed is known to be afflicted with four specific genetic disorders. These include eversion of the nictitating membrane, amaurotic idiocy, lymphedema, and subaortic stenosis.

Eversion of the nictitating membrane refers to an outward "scrolling" of the membrane structure located at the inner corners of each eye, commonly referred to as the "third eyelid." Caused by a defective piece of cartilage located within the third eyelid, eversion of the nictitating membrane results in red, swollen, painful eyes in puppies. One or both eyes may be affected. Treatment of this defect involves surgery to correct the anatomic deviations, or to remove the third eyelids in their entirety. This latter solution is the less desirable, since the removal of these structures can adversely affect tear production in some dogs, predisposing them to keratoconjunctivitis sicca, or "dry" eye.

Amaurotic idiocy is a nervous system disorder that appears in affected puppies at around six months of age. It results from an inherent deficiency in a specific enzyme normally found within the cells of the nervous system. This deficiency leads to an abnormal accumulation of nutrients within the cells, eventually leading to cellular malfunction. Clinical signs include nervousness, poor trainability, and behavioral changes. As the disease progresses, affected dogs will become extremely weak, often seizuring and falling into a coma. Unfortunately, there is no treatment for this genetic disease, and those dogs so afflicted will usually die before their second birthday.

Subaortic stenosis, or SAS, is distinguished by a narrowing or obstruction of the passage through which blood exits the heart and enters general circulation. This narrowing is caused by the presence of fibrous scar tissue near the heart valve that controls the flow of blood through the passage. The increased workload placed on the heart by the obstruction eventually leads to a thickening of the heart wall and heart failure. Symptoms will develop in affected puppies within the first month of life, and can include stunted growth, weakness, shortness of breath, abdominal swelling, and, in extreme instances, sudden death. Medical treatment is directed toward decreasing the workload on the diseased heart. Surgical correction of the defect may be attempted, yet owing to the nature of the disease and the age of affected patients, the outcome of such a procedure is generally poor.

Finally, lymphedema is a genetic defect characterized by the abnormal accumulation of lymph fluid within the tissue of the body, especially within the fatty tissue found just beneath the skin surface. Lymphedema results from a malformation of the vessels that carry this special fluid (which contains absorbed fats and immune cells) throughout the body. Proper drainage of lymph from the tissues is denied, leading to swollen, nonpainful legs and scarring within affected tissues. Symptoms of this disorder may be noticeable at birth, or develop within the first few months of life. Unfortunately, as with most genetically based diseases, there is no effective treatment for lymphedema. Most puppies suffering from severe cases will eventually die. Those experiencing milder involvement will usually live, yet experience a reduced quality of life.

Degenerative Diseases

These diseases include those associated with normal wear and tear due to age, such as certain forms of kidney and heart disease. Although most occur due to age, not all degenerative diseases follow the same pattern. For instance, arthritis can result from years of continuous wear and tear on the joints due to hunting, or it can develop rapidly following an acute joint injury. In most instances, degenerative diseases are difficult to treat, with management geared toward slowing the progression of the condition and alleviating clinical signs rather than achieving a cure.

Hip dysplasia is a degenerative disease that involves the hip joints of affected dogs. It can also be classified as an inherited disease, since genetics plays a role in its transmission. The disease is characterized by a malformation and abnormal articulation of one or both hip joints, resulting in degeneration and erosion of the joint cartilage and bony surfaces. Although the incidence of hip dysplasia in the German Shorthaired Pointer is much lower than that for many of its retriever

counterparts, when it occurs, it can have devastating consequences. Hip dysplasia can manifest itself suddenly in the young dog, or may gradually appear over time as the dog matures. In younger dogs, severe pain and lameness can result. In older dogs, a gradual onset of pain and lameness, with restricted joint movement is often the typical presentation.

Diagnosis of hip dysplasia is achieved by radiographing (X-ray) suspected joints and from a history of this disorder in the dog's genetic bloodline. Treatment for this condition consists of moderate daily exercise to help strengthen the muscles and tendons underlying and supporting the affected joint, and anti-inflammatory medications to help relieve any pain that may be present. In severe cases of osteoarthrosis, surgical intervention may be required to clean and re-build the joints in an attempt to restore relatively pain-free function. Also, promising results have been obtained using drugs like polysulfated glycosaminoglycan (PSGAG) in dogs suffering from the ravages of this disease. PSGAG works to stimulate and encourage the repair of damaged joint cartilage, thereby effectively relieving the pain associated with bone-to-bone contact.

Because many cases of hip dysplasia don't become apparent until a later age, several diagnostic methods exist for identifying the disease in younger dogs, before the appearance of symptoms. The Orthopedic Foundation for Animals Inc. (OFA) has established guidelines for testing and detecting hip dysplasia in dogs two years of age or older. Radiographs of the dog's hip joints are taken by a veterinarian and sent to OFA for review. If no evidence of dysplasia exists on the radiographs, the OFA will certify the dog as free of the condition. Whenever purchasing a German Shorthaired Pointer, ask the seller if the puppy's parents have their

Internal parasitism can quickly lead to malnourishment in the active hunting dog.

resulting in abnormalities in hormone production and/or metabolic processes within the body. Diabetes mellitus and Cushings disease are examples of disorders of the body's normal metabolism due to abnormal hormone production, the former involving insulin production and the latter involving steroid production. Metabolic diseases can manifest themselves outwardly with a wide variety of clinical signs, and can be easily overlooked as the underlying cause of the symptoms. In fact, many metabolic diseases cannot be detected just by a physical exam alone; thorough laboratory work-up is required in most cases to confirm or rule out such a diagnosis.

Hypothyroidism is a metabolic disease that occurs relatively infrequently in German Shorthaired Pointers, yet when it does occur, it can certainly disrupt hunting performance and adversely affect the quality of life of your dog. Thyroid hormone is produced by the thyroid gland, which is located near the base of the neck. This hormone functions to enhance the utilization of nutrients and oxygen within the body, thereby driving metabolism. If a deficiency in this hormone occurs, a state of hypothyroidism is said to exist.

The causes of hypothyroidism can include immune system disorders, iodine deficiencies, and malfunctions of the pituitary gland. Clinical signs include lethargy, exercise intolerance, and intolerance to environmental temperature fluctuations. These dogs tend to gain weight despite poor appetites. Over half of all dogs suffering from hypothyroidism exhibit skin and hair coat changes. A generalized thinning of the coat takes place, the skin thickens and tends to "droop," and secondary seborrhea usually appears. Advanced cases of hypothyroidism can also lead to vision loss, nerve disorders, and joint inflammation if it is not treated properly.

OFA certification. It is just one more bit of reassurance that your new puppy comes to you free of disease.

PennHIP is the name given to a new scientific method of predicting the appearance of hip dysplasia in young dogs. PennHIP has been used to estimate the susceptibility for hip dysplasia in dogs as young as four months of age. Such a tool is especially useful in controlling the spread of the disease, since genetically affected dogs can be identified and rendered sterile before they reach puberty and can pass the unwanted genes to any offspring. The PennHIP technique uses radiographs to measure the degree of tightness in which the hip joints fit together. Those puppies found to possess a certain degree of joint laxity are deemed to be at high risk of developing hip dysplasia. When purchasing a German Shorthaired Pointer puppy sixteen weeks of age or older, you may want to consider having such a test performed to ensure the soundness of your future hunter.

Metabolic Diseases

Metabolic diseases are caused by organ malfunctions within the body,

Hypothyroidism can be easily diagnosed using simple blood testing procedures. If diagnosed, treatment of this disorder entails the administration of synthetic thyroid hormone in liquid or tablet form on a daily basis. Retesting should be performed within six weeks after commencing treatment to ensure that the dosage being given is correct. In most cases, this supplementation will need to be continued for the remainder of your dog's life.

Immune-Mediated Diseases

Allergies are types of immune-mediated diseases in which the body overreacts to the presence of a foreign substance and causes an "allergic reaction." More severe autoimmune diseases, such as autoimmune hemolytic anemia and pemphigus, can actually cause tissue damage and organ failure if not brought under control in a timely manner by medication.

Inhalant allergies can be initiated by breathing air containing grass and tree pollens, molds, dander, house dust, and hair. Signs of this type of allergy include face rubbing, licking and chewing at the feet, scratching behind the elbows and shoulders, and symmetrical hair loss. Small red bumps may be noticeable on the skin of affected dogs, and secondary skin infections due to biting and scratching can occur. Because the ear canals of allergic dogs often become inflamed, as well, ear infections can result.

Diagnosis of inhalant allergies is made using clinical signs (i.e. seasonal versus nonseasonal), response to treatment, and/or allergy testing. This latter testing may involve actual injections of potential allergy-causing agents into the skin and observing for reactions (intradermal testing) or less reliably, evaluation of blood serum samples for antibodies to offending agents. Traditionally, steroid anti-inflammatory drugs have proven most useful in the control of the clinical signs associated with inhalant allergies. However, because long-term continuous use can cause deleterious side effects one or more of the other modes of treatment should be considered. Oral administration of antihistamine medications, combined with omega-3 fatty acid therapy and weekly medicated shampoos, can provide a satisfactory substitute for steroid therapy in many German Shorthaired Pointers. For others, hyposensitization injections containing extracts of the substance(s) identified by intradermal testing as causing the allergy can be successfully given to condition the body to ignore the presence of the offending substance.

The itching and hair loss seen with a flea allergy is the result of an allergic response by the body to flea saliva deposited into the skin. Obviously, flea control is the treatment of choice for this disorder. In addition, the same type of treatments used to control inhalant allergies can be used to help reduce clinical signs associated with flea allergies.

Hypoglycemia can strike dogs that are working hard in the field.

HOW-TO: Performing First Aid on Your German Shorthaired Pointer

Bleeding

To control bleeding, you should immediately apply direct pressure to the source of the hemorrhage. Any readily available absorbent material or object can be used as a compress, including gauze, towels, or shirts. Pressure should be applied for no less than five minutes. If bleeding still persists after this time period, secure the compress using gauze, a belt, pantyhose, or a necktie and seek veterinary help immediately. If an extremity is involved, pressure applied to the inside, upper portion of the affected leg will also reduce blood flow to the limb. If needed, a tourniquet may be applied just above the wound, using a belt, necktie, or pantyhose. A pencil, ruler, or wooden spoon can be used to twist and tighten the tourniquet until bleeding has been minimized. To prevent permanent

Apply direct pressure to bleeding wounds.

Table 5: Items to Include in a First-aid Kit

- Antibiotic Cream or Ointment
- Bandage Scissors
- Betadine Solution
- Cotton Balls
- Digital Thermometer
- Elastic Bandages
- Hydrogen Peroxide 3% solution
- Saline Solution
- Snake Bite Kit
- Sterile Non-stick Dressings
- Sterile Ophthalmic Ointment
- Tongue Depressors
- Tourniquet
- Tweezers
- Two-inch Adhesive Tape
- Two-inch Gauze Roll

damage to the limb, be sure you are able to pass one finger between the tourniquet and the skin without too much effort. In addition, release tourniquet pressure for 30 seconds every ten to fifteen minutes until veterinary care is obtained.

Poisonings

General symptoms associated with a poisoning include vomiting, diarrhea, unconsciousness, seizures, abdominal pain, excessive salivation, panting, and/or shock. Common sources of poisoning in dogs include house plants, rodent poisons, insecticides, chocolate, ethylene glycol (anti-freeze), drug overdose, and ingestion of spoiled or denatured food.

Goals of first-aid treatment for poisoning should be geared toward diluting or neutralizing the poison as much as possible prior to veterinary intervention. If the poison originated from a container, always read and follow the label directions concerning accidental poisoning. In addition, be sure to take the label and container with you to your veterinarian.

If your dog has ingested a caustic or petroleum-based substance, or is severely depressed, seizuring, or unconscious, waste no time in seeking veterinary help. Treatment in these instances should be administered only under a veterinarian's guidance.

For other ingested poisons, induce vomiting using a teaspoon per ten pounds of body weight of hydrogen peroxide or ½ ml. per pound syrup of ipecac. Repeat the dosage of hydrogen peroxide in five minutes if needed.

Following evacuation of the stomach, administer two cups of water orally to help dilute any remaining poison. If available, administer activated charcoal (mix 25 grams of powder in water to form a slurry, then administer one ml. per pound of body weight) or whole milk (one cup) to help deactivate any residual poison.

If the poison was applied to the skin, flush the affected areas with copious amounts of water. If the offending substance is oil based, a quick bath using water plus a mechanic's hand cleaner or dishwashing liquid should be given to remove any remaining residue.

In all instances of poisoning, specific antidotes may be available at your veterinarian's office. As a result, always seek out professional care following initial first-aid efforts.

Bone Fractures

Signs of a fractured bone will include abnormal limb position or mobility, localized pain, bruising and/or crepitation (the crackling feel made when two ends of bone rub together). If the fracture is open, that is, the ends of the bone are protruding through the skin, do not attempt to replace the exposed ends of bone or clean the wound. Control any bleeding that may be present and apply a clean or sterile bandage to the site prior to transporting your dog to your veterinarian. If the fracture is closed and is suspected below the dog's elbow or knee, immobilize it by applying a splint to the affected region. A rolled-up magazine affixed to the limb with adhesive tape or cloth makes an excellent splint. Other materials that can be used as splints include sticks, rulers, and small boards. Be careful not to apply any tape directly over the fracture site. Once the fracture is splinted, carefully transport your Shorthair to your veterinarian at once for further stabilization.

Snakebite

Consequences associated with snakebite are related to the type of snake involved, the amount of venom injected into

Table 6: Normal Physiologic Values for the Shorthair

Temperature	Pulse (beats per minute)	Respirations (per minute)
99.5–102.2°F (37.5–39°C)	60–120	14–22

the dog, and the location of the bite. Signs include obvious puncture wounds, pain, swelling, breathing difficulties, shock, and paralysis. The venom of pit vipers, such as rattlesnakes and water moccasins, causes tissue damage and destroys red blood cells. On the contrary, coral snake venom often causes little pain or swelling; however, it does affect the dog's nervous system, with swallowing difficulties, depression, paralysis, and death common consequences.

Bites that occur on the head and neck can be more serious

Applying a temporary splint using a rolled-up magazine and gauze.

since they can cause direct damage to many vital structures in these regions and interfere with breathing. Furthermore, bites in these areas are difficult to manage by conventional first-aid means. Regardless of the location of the bite, initiate first-aid measures immediately.

If you have a snakebite kit handy, follow the enclosed instructions. Do your best to keep your dog calm to prevent the rapid spread of venom throughout the bloodstream. If you do not have a snakebite kit, and the bite is on an extremity, apply a tourniquet two to three inches above the bite wound. Roll gauze, rubber tubing, belts, neckties, and pantyhose all make good tourniquets for this purpose. Tighten the tourniquet using a stick, pencil, or similar object. The tourniquet should be tight, yet you should still be able to easily slip a finger between it and the skin. Seek veterinary help immediately. Loosen the tourniquet for 30 seconds every 15 minutes (or sooner if the limb begins to swell) until veterinary care is obtained.

Nutritional Diseases

The importance of this category as an underlying cause of disease in dogs cannot be underestimated. As with humans, nutrition plays a vital (and some say even the number one) role in maintaining healthy organ function, including those making up the immune system. It stands to reason, then, that nutritional deficiencies, whether caused by external or internal factors, can cause devastating disease in themselves. For instance, hypoglycemia, or low blood sugar, can be caused by malnutrition, or it can occur secondary to tumors or seizures. Hypoglycemia in hunting dogs, caused by overexertion and depletion of the body's energy stores, can lead to profound weakness and exhaustion in eager hunters. If blood sugar levels are not corrected in a timely manner, death could result. Hunters should carry a small bottle of honey or corn syrup with them in the field to offer their hunting companion at regular intervals if their dog has a predisposition to this condition.

Nutritional diseases can also be caused by a malfunctioning digestive system. Disruptions in the body's ability to absorb nutrients from the ration eaten can have the same effects as if the food wasn't eaten at all. Dogs that are having difficulty putting on weight, or those who underperform even when fed a high-quality ration should be evaluated by your pet health-care professional. Detecting a problem early on will prevent lasting long-term effects.

Feeding your German Shorthair a high-quality ration (devoid of table scraps) on a consistent basis is the cornerstone of disease prevention. Proper nutrition enhances the immune system, improves organ function and body processes, and makes your dog feel good. In contrast, poor nutrition can interfere with organ function, depress the immune system, make muscles, bones, and joints more prone to injury, and significantly reduce the performance of your hunter.

Neoplastic Diseases

Neoplasia becomes an important differential diagnosis to consider in any disease affecting an older animal. This is not to say, however, that younger dogs can't be stricken with this before their time. The term neoplasia refers to the uncontrolled, progressive proliferation of cells within the body. Bypassing the body's normal mechanisms for controlling growth, neoplastic cells reproduce at abnormal rates, often coalescing into firm, distinct masses called tumors. Neoplasia can be classified as either benign or malignant (cancerous), depending upon the behavior of the cells involved.

Cancer in dogs acts in the same way as it does in people, and depending upon which organ system is involved, can present itself as a wide variety of clinical signs and symptoms. Benign neoplasia can cause damage just by sheer size and mechanical disruption; malignant neoplasia can spread throughout the body and affect many organs at once.

Diagnosis of a neoplastic disorder can be accomplished using clinical signs, laboratory testing, radiology, ultrasound, and/or tumor biopsy. Treatment options for neoplasms include surgical removal of defined tumors, radiation therapy (utilizing ionizing radiation to kill malignant neoplasms), chemotherapy (using specific drugs to destroy neoplastic cells), cryotherapy (freezing tumors to kill neoplastic cells), and immunotherapy (injecting substances in order to stimulate and support the body's immune system in its fight against the tumors). While other forms of therapy do exist, such as hyperthermia and anti-platelet therapy, their use in veterinary medicine is limited. A combination of surgery, radiation, and chemotherapy is currently the most favored protocol for treating especially difficult malignancies in dogs. As one may expect, the earlier a cancer is detected, the greater the chances are for complete cure.

Although German Shorthaired Pointers can be stricken with several different types of cancer, there are two types that are worth mentioning here due to a higher-than-normal frequency in the breed. These are fibrosarcomas and melanomas. Fibrosarcomas are malignant tumors arising from the fibrous tissue located just beneath the skin. They are usually present as solitary, irregular masses on or protruding from the skin, especially in the flank, groin, and limb regions. Metastasis (spread) to the lungs and lymph nodes is common. Diagnosis of fibrosarcomas is made through biopsy evaluation. Treatment involves a combination of surgery, radiation therapy, and cryotherapy. Unfortunately, fibrosarcomas are generally resistant to most forms of chemotherapy, rendering this treatment option impotent.

Melanomas are neoplasms that originate from pigmented cells of the skin, with a special predilection for the lips, tongue, gums, oral cavity, eyelids, and the digits of the feet. The degree of malignancy exhibited by these tumors seems to be directly correlated with where they are located. For example, melanomas involving the mouth and oral cavity tend to be more malignant than those affecting the digits or eyelids. Benign or slow-growing melanomas appear as darkly pigmented nodules or skin blotches with well-defined borders. Rarely do they exceed one inch in diameter. Malignant melanomas, on the other hand, appear as rapidly growing, often ulcerated masses or nodules that may or may not be pigmented and can reach greater sizes. These cancers often metastasize via the blood and lymph to various organs throughout the body,

Snakebites can pose a threat to Shorthairs in the field, particularly in the southern United States.

including the liver, lungs, spleen, brain, spinal cord, heart, and bone. Definitive diagnosis of a melanoma and whether or not a malignancy exists is accomplished through biopsy and microscopic examination of the tumor. Radiography, ultrasonography, and lymph-node biopsies may all be used to help determine the extent of metastasis if a malignancy is diagnosed. Treatment involves the surgical removal of the tumor and radiation therapy. As with fibrosarcomas, chemotherapy has proven to be of limited use in the treatment of malignant melanoma. Unfortunately, malignant melanomas have usually undergone metastasis by the time they are first recognized, and tend to recur after surgical removal. As a result, an overall prognosis for cure is poor.

Infectious/Parasitic Diseases

In dogs, this classification of disease has the highest incidence of all the others combined. A multitude of viral, bacterial, and fungal organisms can infect dogs and cause disease, especially in those dogs allowed to roam and interact indiscriminately with other animals and who have not been properly vaccinated. Intestinal parasites are also very common in dogs, and, besides gastrointestinal upset, can cause skin disorders, malnutrition, and immune system suppression. External parasites, such as fleas, can carry with them their share of health problems as well. Demodectic mange is an example of a parasitic disease that would also fall into the category of congenital, or inherited disease, since German Shorthaired Pointers affected by this parasite usually have a poor immune function.

In recent years, Lyme disease has come to the forefront in public awareness due to its ability to cause human illness. The disease, caused by the bacterium *Borrelia burgdorferi*, is primarily spread to dogs and to humans through the bite of an infected tick. Many different species of ticks can be involved, including the deer tick, the black-legged tick, and the Western blacklegged tick. Ticks, however, are not the only way the disease can be spread; fleas and other biting insects are capable of its spread as well. In addition, there have even been incidents in which Lyme disease has been transmitted via direct contact with infected body fluids. Because of this ease of transmission, Lyme disease is one of the most commonly reported tick-borne diseases, and has been diagnosed in most states across the country. Because of the greater potential for exposure to infected ticks, hunting dogs like the German Short-

haired Pointer have an increased risk of contracting this malady.

Clinical signs of Lyme disease in dogs include loss of appetite, lethargy, high fever, swollen lymph nodes and joints, and/or a sudden onset of lameness. This lameness often resolves on its own accord, only to re-occur weeks to months later. In untreated dogs, kidney disease and heart disease can be an unfortunate sequel. Diagnosis is based upon a history of exposure to ticks and of recurring lameness. Veterinarians now have the ability to test for this disease in-house, affording a rapid confirmation or denial of the suspected diagnosis. Rapid treatment of a diagnosed case of Lyme disease is essential to prevent permanent damage to the joints or internal organs. Many different types of antibiotics can be used to treat this disease, and acute signs will usually disappear within 36 hours of instituting such therapy. Long-standing infections may not respond as well, and require a more vigorous treatment approach.

A vaccine against Lyme disease is now available for use in dogs and should be given to your German Shorthaired Pointer if it hunts in high risk areas. After the initial immunization, a booster is recommended three weeks later, followed thereafter by annual revaccination. Tick control is another important measure to prevent Lyme disease. Since a tick must feed for about 24 hours before spread of the disease will take place, prompt removal of ticks will help break the transmission cycle.

Breeding Your German Shorthaired Pointer

A sound knowledge of canine reproductive principles constitutes the livelihood of the professional breeder of German Shorthaired Pointers. But professional breeders are not the only ones that need to know about these matters; owners desiring to breed their German Shorthaired Pointers must also do their homework prior to proceeding with such plans. For this purpose, this chapter will come in quite handy.

To begin, a brief overview of the anatomical and functional features of the canine reproductive system, both male and female, will aid in understanding the principles behind reproduction in German Shorthaired Pointers. Beginning with the male, or sire, the major parts of the reproductive system include the testes (testicles), with associated epididymis and ductus deferens, the scrotum, the penis, containing the urethra, and the prostate gland.

The testes are the organs responsible for the production of spermatozoa. This production is directly influenced by the hormone testosterone, also produced by the testes. Aside from regulating sperm production, testosterone affects normal male sexual behavior, territorial behavior, and hunting behavior. Normally, the testicles should descend into the scrotum shortly after birth, usually no later than eight weeks of age. If this event fails to occur, the dog is said to be "cryptorchid," and surgical removal of the testicles is indicated to prevent medical problems in the future and to prevent the passage of that undesirable trait to offspring.

From the testicle, sperm is shunted into the epididymis, a structure closely attached to each testicle, where it finishes its maturation process. Upon copulation, the mature sperm is transported from the epididymis through the ductus deferens and to the tubelike urethra coursing within the penis. The canine penis has the uncommon ability to swell near its origin during erection, effecting the unique interlocking "tie" with the female during reproduction. In addition, the latter half of the dog's penis contains a bony structure called the os penis, which is grooved underneath to allow for the passage of the urethra.

The prostate gland, considered an accessory sex gland, is located surrounding the urethra near the neck of the bladder. It functions to produce prostatic fluid, which mixes with sperm to form semen, and helps to increase the survivability of the sperm within the female reproductive tract. Enlargement or inflammation of this gland is not uncommon as intact male dogs mature. Constipation, discharges from the penis, and painful urination can be clinical signs of a prostatic disorder.

The major reproductive organs of the female dog, or bitch, include the ovaries, the oviducts, the uterus, the vagina, and the vulva. The ovaries are responsible for the production and release of eggs destined to be fertilized by the male sperm. In addition, several important reproductive

Breeding your German Shorthaired Pointer can have its rewards.

The Reproductive Cycle

Puberty is defined as the age in which female German Shorthaired Pointers first come into heat, and when the male testicle first begins to produce spermatozoa. On the average though, German Shorthaired Pointers reach puberty around eight to ten months of age. However, just because puberty is reached does not mean that he or she has reached breeding age.

As a general rule, you should wait until your male dog reaches at least 12 to 14 months before using him for breeding purposes; for female German Shorthaired Pointers, breeding attempts should not be made until the second or third heat cycle. Even these guidelines may vary some, depending on the dog's level of maturity, both mental and physical.

The optimum breeding age for female German Shorthaired Pointers is between three and six years. Puppies born to females in these age groups tend to be healthier at birth, fast growers, and wean much easier when compared to others. After six years, reproductive performance in the female begins a steady decline. Male dogs, on the other hand, have greater sexual longevity than do females, yet this too begins to decline as the dog advances in years.

The estrous cycle is the series of events that occurs within the female reproductive tract between actual heat periods. On the average, this cycle lasts from six to eight months. There are four phases to this cycle, including anestrus, proestrus, estrus, and metestrus.

Anestrus is the period of time in which there is no reproductive activity going on in the ovaries at all. The duration of anestrus is typically four to five months. From anestrus, the reproductive cycle enters the period of proestrus. Signs seen during proestrus are related to an increased production of the hormone estrogen

hormones are produced by these structures. Unfertilized eggs are released, or ovulated, by the ovaries, and pass into the small oviducts. It is within these oviducts that fertilization, if impending, takes place. After this is accomplished, the fertilized egg, or embryo, continues its passage down the oviducts on its way to the uterus.

When an embryo reaches the uterus, it attaches itself to the uterine wall and begins its development. If fertilization has not taken place, this attachment won't take place and the egg is eventually absorbed by the body.

The uterus is separated from the vagina by a ring of muscle known as the cervix. Most of the time, this cervix remains open. During pregnancy, however, the cervix will close, preventing outside access to the uterine environment. Then, at time of parturition, the cervix relaxes, allowing the birth to take place. Finally, the external opening of the vagina is termed the vulva. As a dog enters into her heat cycle, the vulva will begin to noticeably swell, tipping owners off to the impending heat.

by the ovaries, and include vaginal bleeding, and a gradual swelling of the vulvae. Proestrus can last anywhere from seven to fourteen days. Normally, female German Shorthaired Pointers will not stand to be mated until the waning days of this phase.

As vaginal bleeding subsides and proestrus ends, estrus, or true heat, begins (the term "estrus" should not be confused with "estrous cycle"). As with proestrus, this heat period can last one to two weeks, and is characterized by sexual receptivity of the bitch to the sire and by ovulation of unfertilized eggs from the ovaries. A common misconception among novice dog owners is that once a dog begins to bleed, she is "in heat." In actuality, they are just beginning proestrus and have yet to reach this stage. Another interesting fact about the heat period in the dog is that eggs that are ovulated from the ovaries may mature and become fertilizable at different rates. As a result, it is possible for mixed litters to occur if the female dog happens to be bred by more than one male.

The last stage in the estrous cycle is metestrus, which can last from two to three months. It is said to begin when the female refuses to still accept the sire for breeding. It is the period of uterine repair, or if fertilization is achieved, the period of pregnancy.

False pregnancies can appear during this metestrual phase. When the ovaries of a female dog release eggs to be fertilized, they then start to produce a hormone called progesterone. Now the function of progesterone is to maintain pregnancy if egg fertilization occurs. However, a unique feature about dogs is that even if fertilization does not occur, progesterone levels will remain high for up to ten weeks after heat is over. It is precisely this behavior that is responsible for the condition dog owners know as pseudopregnancy, or false pregnancy.

All female dogs exhibit some form of pseudopregnancy after they come out of heat. In most, signs associated with it go unnoticed by the owner. However, some dogs do exhibit marked changes as a result of these high progesterone levels, including mammary gland enlargement with or without the production of milk, and behavioral changes that include restlessness, nesting, mothering of inanimate objects, and loss of appetite. In short, they may actually appear to be expectant mothers! Oftentimes, without the use of ultrasound or radiographic x-rays, there is no way to be sure that they are not.

The Breeding Process

As your German Shorthaired Pointer approaches her estrus, several different signs will be noticed. First, the vaginal discharge changes from a red color to a brown or tan color as estrus arrives. Secondly, her vulvae will turn flaccid in appearance as she comes into heat. Finally, females entering into estrus will often flag their tails; that is, they move the tail to the side of the body when touched around the rear end.

Many breeders begin counting days once proestrual bleeding appears. Usually by day ten after this bleeding starts, the female becomes willing to accept a male dog and attempts should be made to breed. If the female refuses to mate at this time, wait two days and try again. After the first mating occurs, a second mating should be performed three to four days later.

Your veterinarian can be quite helpful in your decision about the best time to breed your German Shorthaired Pointer about to enter into heat. By microscopically examining slides containing smears of vaginal cells, she can pinpoint the exact dates when proestrus and estrus begin.

This information is especially helpful for those female dogs who tend to exhibit subtle proestrual and estrual signs. In these, and in others, this vaginal cytology is an invaluable aid toward ensuring correct timing when it comes to matings.

When deciding where exactly the breeding should take place, remember that it is better to take the female dog to the male's own environment, rather than vice versa. Males tend to feel more comfortable in their own territory, and will perform their duties with less problems and distractions.

The male and female should be introduced to each other restrained by leashes and with owners present. That way, if personality conflicts arise, they can be quickly quelled before a fight breaks out (such conflicts may arise if the female is not yet ready to accept a male). If the two seem compatible, then breeding can be allowed to take place. Some experts recommend muzzling both dogs prior to breeding to prevent accidental injuries or personality surges. Whether you actually stick around for the mating is up to you; some of the more inexperienced dogs may need assistance. Most dogs don't mind the presence of a third party, though it may make some uncomfortable with the situation. A key point to remember is that once mounting takes place, it's best to leave the two alone from then on. After mounting, the two will "lock" together, forming what is termed a "tie." While intercourse is maintained via the tie, the male may manipulate himself around so that both dogs' posteriors are facing each other, with their heads pointed in opposite directions. This is a normal mating position, and dogs so locked together should not be disturbed until the mating process has been voluntarily completed. Normal ties will last from ten to thirty minutes, although longer ones are not uncom-

mon. After the tie is released by the male, the two will separate, and breeding is complete.

Occasionally, you'll find that some dogs cannot breed properly due to personality problems or physical defects. In these cases, artificial insemination offers a viable way to obtain a litter from your Shorthair.

Care of the Pregnant Pointer

Pregnancy in dogs ranges from 59 to 65 days, with the average being 63 days. Ultrasonography provides a reliable way to confirm pregnancy status as early as 28 days. If an ultrasound is not available, abdominal palpation by trained hands can often achieve similar results. However, there is much room for error with this method, especially if the female dog is tense during the examination. Abdominal enlargement and mammary development usually become noticeable after the first month of pregnancy. If uncertainty still exists, X-rays can be used to confirm pregnancies as early as 42 days.

Care of your pregnant Pointer consists of nothing more than maintaining a good plane of nutrition and reducing stress as much as possible. Pregnant bitches should be placed on a growth-type ration, similar to those used for puppies, during pregnancy and lactation. Vitamin and mineral supplements are generally not required. Moderate exercise (i.e., two fifteen-minute walks daily) is certainly acceptable and encouraged during your dog's pregnancy. However, hunting and intense activity should be avoided.

While your dog is pregnant, administer all medications only upon your veterinarian's direct consent or under her direct supervision. Many drugs can harm both mother and unborn pups if given during pregnancy. Always check the labels on insecticidal products used for flea and tick control before applying them to pregnant dogs. The label should state whether or not that product is safe to use on pregnant pets. If it doesn't say anything about it at all, play it safe: Don't use it. Heartworm prevention medications on the market are safe for use during pregnancy and can be used without interruption.

Parturition (Whelping)

As mentioned previously, the average length of pregnancy in the dog is 63 days. It is important to record the breeding date in order to accurately predict when parturition will occur in your Pointer. You will want to provide your dog a special area or enclosure, complete with clean towels, in which to build her "nest." Allow her at least three weeks prior to the due date to become familiar and comfortable with this whelping site.

Interestingly enough, the season of the year can affect what time during the day that your dog will whelp. For instance, during the spring and summer months, whelping tends to occur during the early morning hours. On the contrary, whelping during the fall and winter months commonly occur in the late afternoon or evening hours.

Twelve to twenty-four hours before parturition, the rectal temperature of your dog will drop to as low as 97°F (36°C). Additionally, a yellow, gelatinous discharge may appear up to two days before whelping. These signs should alert you of impending parturition.

Parturition can be divided into three stages. Stage one (pre-labor) may last anywhere from two to 36 hours. Signs associated with this stage include pacing, anxiety, nest-building, loss of appetite, vomiting, and/or shivering. Stage two (true labor) is characterized by straining, abdominal contractions, the appearance of the placental sac, and the actual birth of a puppy. Stage three (expulsion) marks the passage

of the placenta, either with the puppy at birth or soon thereafter. A greenish fluid should accompany a normal delivery.

Don't feel you must intervene in nature's process. Leave your dog alone in her quiet, stress-free environment to do her business. Many dogs will actually delay parturition if disturbed by the unnecessary presence of an owner. Fortunately, as a breed, German Shorthaired Pointers rarely run into problems with parturition. When should you get concerned about the process? Use the following guidelines to help you determine if a phone call to your veterinarian is warranted. Contact your veterinarian if:

1. Your dog's pregnancy has lasted more than 63 days

2. A black or red, foul-smelling discharge is noted

3. Stage one labor has lasted more than 36 hours

4. More than two hours has elapsed since the onset of stage two labor and no puppy has been born

5. Greater than three hours elapses between births

6. The mother fails to remove the placental membranes from around the puppy's head (Go ahead and remove them yourself.)

7. The mother fails to sever the umbilical cord of the pup (Tie off the cord with thin gauze or thread by making a knot about one-half inch from the body wall of the puppy, then sever the cord between the tie and the membranes. Treat the end of the umbilical stump with tamed iodine.)

8. The puppy hasn't started breathing within one minute after birth

Following delivery and clean-up by the mother, newborn puppies will usually find their way to her milk supply. Keep an eye out for puppies that are being rejected and ignored by your female for one reason or another. For instance, this rejection may occur if

As pregnancy progresses, the mammary glands will begin to swell and fill with milk.

pies will eat, move around, and sleep. Crying usually indicates hunger, and should cease when the puppy is allowed to nurse. If you notice any variations in this behavior, it is time to intervene and call your veterinarian.

Hypoglycemia (low blood sugar) can result from lack of intake of mother's milk. It is often seen in puppies too weak to nurse. This condition requires immediate attention, for it can lead to profound weakness, convulsions, and death. Commercially available formulas are ideal milk substitutes. The amounts you need to feed are printed on the label. However, in emergency situations, a homemade formula can be prepared and used for puppies. It consists of one large egg yolk and enough homogenized milk to make four to six ounces of formula. The mixture may be sweetened by adding one teaspoon of honey to eight ounces of formula. This homemade formula can be fed according to the willingness of the puppy to accept the formula. A general rule of thumb is one tablespoon of formula per two ounces of the animal's body weight every 24 hours. For example, a six-ounce puppy would get three tablespoons of formula in 24 hours. Feedings should be performed every two hours. You can obtain a feeding syringe or pet nurser from your veterinarian or local pet store. If the neonate simply refuses to eat, tube feeding may be required. Ask your veterinarian for details. It should be emphasized that this formula is only for emergencies, and the commercial formula should be started as soon as possible.

Diarrhea is a very dangerous condition in neonatal German Shorthairs. Sometimes, the only sign of diarrhea you'll notice is an inflamed rectum, since mothers are so good at cleaning up after their young. Toxic-milk syndrome is one of the diseases that can cause diarrhea in neonates. Toxic milk

the newborn's body temperature is lower than normal, if it happens to be the runt of the litter, or if it has any physical abnormalities.

If you suspect rejection, warm the puppy using a blanket or well-insulted heating pad (use low setting only!), then place it back with its mother and the rest of the litter. If this does not work, you may need to hand-feed the puppy yourself. Contact your veterinarian for instructions.

It is wise to have your dog checked by your veterinarian as soon as you think all the puppies have been delivered. An entire litter is usually born within twelve hours after the onset of parturition (this can vary greatly). A dark red discharge may be seen from the vulvae following the last birth.

Care of Newborn Puppies

German Shorthaired Pointers exhibit proficient maternal instincts and rarely require assistance in the care of their offspring. However, there are select instances in which intervention on your part is indicated. For the most part, normal, healthy, contented pup-

may result if mastitis (mammary gland infection) or uterine infection exists in the mother. Affected neonates often bloat suddenly, cry frequently, have elevated temperatures, and are restless. When toxic-milk syndrome is suspected, neonates must be prevented from nursing from the mother, and your veterinarian should be contacted.

A puppy's hydration status may be easily evaluated by testing the elasticity of the skin over its back. If the skin fails to fall back to its natural position after being pulled up with your fingers, the puppy may be dehydrated. Contact the veterinarian if you notice this sign. Since puppies can dehydrate seven times faster than adult dogs, this condition can prove to be fatal rapidly if not treated immediately.

Another common cause of death in puppies is hypothermia (abnormally low body temperature). This condition is often seen in neonates rejected by their mothers. To help prevent hypothermia, the air temperature should be maintained at or above 70°F (21°C) at all times and care should be taken to prevent the young from being exposed to drafts and to cold floors.

Finally, orphaned or neglected puppies less than three to four weeks of age have a tendency to retain urine and feces, since they aren't being stimulated to eliminate by their mother. To help these pups perform these necessary functions, they should be gently massaged in the genital area with a cotton ball soaked with warm water until elimination takes place. This should be performed immediately after each feeding and once again before the next feeding.

Tail Docking and Dewclaw Removal

Established conformational standards dictate that select breeds of dogs, including German Shorthaired Pointers, have artificially shortened

Hypoglycemia can pose a threat if a puppy is prevented from nursing by its littermates.

tails and be free of dewclaws. Tail docking originated in centuries past as a way to prevent hunting and sporting dogs from traumatizing their tails while working in thick woods or underbrush.

Dewclaws are actually functionless remnants of the first digit on each paw. Many puppies are born without any dewclaws at all; others may be born with them on the front paws, but not the back, or vice versa. Dewclaws have a nasty habit of getting snagged and torn on carpet, furniture, and in sporting dogs like German Shorthaired Pointers, underbrush. Secondary infections can develop if this trauma is repeated. For this reason, removal of dewclaws is indicated.

Tail docking and dewclaw removal are best performed within the first week of life, and simply involve snipping off the dewclaws and the desired length of tail (per breed standards) with scissors. One to two sutures are usually placed in the tail; the site of the dewclaw removal is often cauterized and left open to heal. If tail docking and dewclaw removal are not performed within seven days after birth, anesthesia will be required for the surgery. As a result, the procedures will have to be postponed until the dog is five to six months of age and can tolerate anesthesia.

Understanding Your German Shorthaired Pointer

Have you ever wondered what your dog is thinking while it is staunchly pointing out that ruffed grouse? How about its behavior? Do you ever wonder why your four-legged friend acts and reacts the way it does? How do you properly approach behavioral problems to ensure their correction? The answers to these questions can be gleaned from an understanding of basic canine behavior, which, apart from certain instinctive controls, is governed by two dominant factors: sensory perception and learning intelligence.

Sensory Perception

As you can guess, dogs perceive their world differently than we do. This is vital to remember, especially when training them, since in our own perception we may not completely understand certain responses and behaviors that we see in them. However, by learning how our friends perceive the world with their senses, the reasons become clearer.

Sight

The visual acuity of the dog has been compared to that of a human's at sunset. They see only generalized forms rather than distinct images or features. Have you ever worn a new hat or sunglasses around your dog, then have it back away or bark in apprehension? Because you changed your features, it was initially unable to recognize you visually; only your scent gave you away. Some dogs exhibit a high degree of nervousness and even aggressiveness around Halloween. The reason: All the "generalized forms" (costumed figures) it has never seen before running from house to house yelling "trick or treat!"

Contrary to popular belief, dogs are not totally colorblind; in fact, the canine eye possesses all of those structures necessary for it to perceive its world in color. Now whether or not the dog takes full advantage of this is still a matter of speculation. It seems, however, that since the sense of sight is not as vital to most dogs as, let's say, the sense of smell, there may be no real need for color perception.

Smell

By far, the most important sense for a dog (especially the hunter) is the sense of smell. The brain of the dog has almost ten times more area devoted to smell than does the human brain. As a result, canine noses are so acute that it's nearly impossible to artificially mask a scent from them. This characteristic has certainly proven useful to man in terms of hunting and tracking. Dogs can also use their noses as homing devices, trailing a weak scent over a considerable distance until it gets stronger and stronger and finally leads the dog to the subject.

The excellent tracking skills of the German Shorthaired Pointer arise from its ability to detect distinct volatile fatty acids or blood located on the skin surface of game or that left over from contact of the surface of that game with the ground, brush, and/or trees. Also, due to its hound ancestry, the German Shorthair may prefer to trail foot scents rather than aerial or body scents. Some will tend to work an area with their heads lowered to the ground, which slows down the speed of the hunt. However, being the versatile breed that it is, some will prefer to begin a hunt with their noses in the air (like their Pointer counterparts), alternating aerial scents with foot scents while tracking down their quarry with extreme accuracy. As a rule, all Shorthairs excel at tracking down wounded running game, using either a foot scent or blood scent.

Hearing

The sense of hearing in the average dog is much more finely tuned than that in a human, allowing it to detect much higher sound pitches at a wider range of frequencies. The upper range of canine hearing is thought to be around 47,000 cycles per second, almost 30,000 cycles per second higher than that for people. Silent dog whistles were invented based on this principle, with the pitch emitted being just above human hearing range but well within that of the dog being summoned. However, the long, pendulous ear flaps of the German Shorthaired Pointer may muffle this pitch at a distance; as a result, silent whistles should not be relied upon for field training. Also, the high pitch emitted by many of the new electronic flea collars available on the market may also fall well within the hearing range of the Shorthair, raising serious questions as to their safe and comfortable use.

Dogs can detect much higher sound pitches and frequencies than can humans.

Taste

Ever wondered why some dogs, when fed table scraps, become incessant beggars? The answer lies in their tongue, which contains a high proportion of taste buds that respond to sugars and certain "sweet" amino acids. In essence, your Shorthair can quickly develop a "sweet tooth" if fed improperly! Some dogs will even go so far as to refuse well-balanced rations for the sweeter "junk" food. The ramifications of this in regard to the health and performance of your hunter are obvious. As a result, to prevent bad habits from forming, avoid the temptation to consistently sneak your pal snacks between meals.

Learning Intelligence

The most basic type of learning exhibited by dogs that will govern their actions is called habituation, which is characterized by a diminishing response to a repeated stimulus over time. Teaching a German Shorthaired Pointer to remain calm in the

The eyesight of the dog has been compared to that of a human's at sunset.

face of gunfire is a classic example of this type of learning put to practical use. A second type of learning that influences behavior is called associative learning, in which the dog creates links between two or more different types of actions, results, and/or stimuli. For instance, rewards given for desired behavior invoke this type of

Even the most well-camouflaged quarry cannot escape the nose of the German Shorthaired Pointer.

learning, creating a strong pleasurable link with the behavior in question, greatly increasing the chances that your dog will repeat the behavior.

Socialization or species imprintation is also thought to be a form of associative learning; however, it undoubtedly involves more complex learning patterns as well, as evidenced by its oftentimes irreversible nature.

There is no doubt that the most important time in the life of your German Shorthaired Pointer puppy is between the ages of three and twelve weeks. During this short timespan, your young hunter will learn who it is, who you are, and who and what all of those other living, moving beings surrounding it are as well. If for some reason a puppy fails to be properly introduced to members of its own species, or to other species as well (including children) during this time, then there is a good chance that it will not "recognize" these individuals for who they are and may even show aggressiveness toward them. For instance, dogs intended for breeding purposes must be properly socialized to members of their own species if they are to be expected to breed easily with one of these members. Good examples of dogs not properly socialized include those that may show extreme aggressiveness to men only, or those aggressive to children.

Dogs see people as two species: big people and little people. As a result, although a dog may recognize an adult person as the one who feeds him and commands it, it may not recognize a small toddler as one who commands the same respect if it has never been properly socialized to small children. Some dogs aren't fit for any type of human interaction at all; they have absolutely no socialization whatsoever and could pose a threat to humans. Fortunately, German Shorthaired Pointers rarely fall into this category.

Another good example of the socialization principle is the relationship between dogs and cats. Dogs and cats that grow up together from the start may be the best of buddies, whereas those that don't may exhibit marked animosity toward one another.

Improper or negative socialization is even worse than no socialization at all. Any traumatic experience or physical punishment that occurs between eight and twelve weeks of age could permanently scar a dog's personality to a specific group or species for life. For instance, many dogs who fear men were actually abused by a member of this gender during this critical socialization time. This is one reason why all physical punishment should be avoided during this time in your puppy's life. Such activity could damage the pup's relationship with the punisher for life!

Whenever purchasing a German Shorthaired Pointer older than 12 weeks of age, question the seller about the puppy's socialization experiences and the specific steps that the seller took to ensure that proper socialization took place. If you don't, you have no way of knowing whether or not proper socialization has taken place, and you may be faced with behavioral problems or poor field performance in the future.

Solving Behavioral Challenges

Nothing can do more to dampen the bond you share with your German Shorthaired Pointer than behavioral challenges. The bad news is that addressing behavioral problems takes time and effort on your part. The good news is that most can be brought under control through the use of special techniques and/or therapy. By allowing your veterinarian to play an active role in the treatment process, you will increase the chances of success a hundredfold!

German Shorthairs are highly intelligent dogs possessing the power of focused concentration.

Proper socialization is vital for positive behavioral development in the puppy.

Separation Anxiety

Have you ever left the house, sometimes for only a few minutes, and your "best friend" proceeds to chew up the furniture, bark or howl, and/or eliminate in the house. If your dog behaves this way when you leave your home, it is probably suffering from the behavioral problem known as "separation anxiety." Before a problem like separation anxiety can be successfully treated, it is helpful to know what causes it.

Dogs are considered "pack animals"; that is, they prefer to run in groups rather than individually. Being its owner, a dog will consider you part of its "pack" and will constantly want to associate with you. When you leave, you separate the dog from its "pack" and this creates separation anxiety. This behavior will be magnified if you tend to make a big fuss over the dog when leaving or returning to the house. Furthermore, certain other behavioral patterns on your part, such as rattling the car keys or turning off the television, can be associated with your departure by the dog.

When treating separation anxiety, one must remember that it is an instinctive behavior; it is not due to disobedience and/or lack of training. As a result, punishment for the act tends to be unrewarding. In fact, most of these dogs would rather be punished than left alone! The key to treating this problem lies in planning short-term departures, then gradually lengthening them until your dog gets used to your absence. Begin by stepping out of the house for only a few seconds (ten to fifteen) at a time for the first few days or so. Hopefully this will allow your dog to get used to you leaving the house, since it will learn that you will return soon. Vary your training session times throughout the day. The idea is to gradually lengthen your leaves of absence (30 seconds at first, then one minute, then two minutes, etc.) so that your departures soon become second nature to the dog.

Points to keep in mind when attempting to break your Shorthair of this annoying behavior are as follows: (1) Don't make a fuss over your dog within five to ten minutes of your arrival to or departure from home. This will help keep the excitement and anxiety levels in your dog to a minimum. (2) During your training sessions, try not to re-enter the house while the dog is performing the undesirable act. Doing so will only serve to positively re-enforce the dog to repeat the act. (3) Eliminate any behavior which may key the dog off to your departure, such as rattling your car keys, saying "goodbye" to your dog, etc. (4) For the dog that likes to chew a lot, provide plenty of nylon chew bones to occupy its time. (5) Leaving the television or radio on while you're gone seems to help in some cases.

In severe cases, veterinarians can prescribe anti-anxiety medications such as amitriptyline-HCl to help assist in the treatment of separation anxiety. As a result, don't hesitate to contact your veterinarian if you are having difficulty in quelling your dog's separation anxiety problem.

Barking

Let's face it: Some dogs just love to hear their own voice! Unfortunately, most owners and their neighbors hardly share the same adoration. There is no doubt that dogs who bark excessively are a nuisance and can cause many a sleepless night. For this reason, correction of the problem is essential to your sanity, and that of those who live around you.

A dog may bark excessively for a number of reasons. The first is boredom. German Shorthaired Pointers that have nothing else to do may simply "sing" to themselves to whittle the time away. Another potential cause is territoriality. Outsiders, be they human or animal, will almost always elicit a bark out of a dog if threatening to encroach upon its territory. Dogs may also use the bark indiscriminately as a communiqué to other outsiders to stay away. In such instances, the barking episode may be tipped off by the far-off baying of a neighborhood dog or the slamming of a car door down the street.

Separation anxiety is another common source of nuisance barking. Some dogs have it so bad that they bark continuously when their owner leaves them, even for a short period of time. Oftentimes, the owner will return home to find their dog hoarse from so much barking.

When attempting to break your dog of this annoying habit, always remember this one principle: If you respond to your dog's barking by yelling at it or physically punishing it, you are going to make the problem worse. Dogs that are isolated from their owners for most of the day don't give a darn about what kind of attention they receive (positive or negative), just as long as they get some. Dogs that are barking out of boredom or from separation anxiety will soon learn that their action will eventually get them attention, and they'll keep doing it. Even dogs that are barking for other reasons can catch on quickly that such vocalization will bring them a bonus of attention from their beloved owners. As a result, no matter how mad you get, or how sleepy you are, avoid the urge to punish your dog for its barking.

The first thing you need to determine is whether or not separation anxiety has anything to do with the problem. If you think it does, treat it as you would any other case of separation anxiety. In many cases, dogs that bark for this reason alone can be broken of their habit. Keep in mind, though, that the source of the barking may involve a combination of the factors, not just one.

German Shorthaired Pointers that bark for other reasons besides separation anxiety need to be given more attention throughout the day. A dog that tends to bark through the night should be given plenty of exercise in the evening to encourage a good night's sleep. A nylon chew bone can be helpful at diverting its attention. Feeding its daily ration later in the evening may also promote contentment for the night.

For those times of the day or night that the barking seems the worst, consider bringing the dog inside the house or inside of the garage. This, of course, may not be possible if you failed to instruct your dog as to the ways of household living when it was a puppy. Nevertheless, removing your dog from its "primary" territory and/or increasing the amount of contact with members of its pack can help curb the urge to bark. Also, if feasible, encourage your neighbors to keep their pets indoors at night, since nighttime roaming activities of neighborhood dogs and cats are major causes of nuisance barking.

House Soiling

It has happened to all of us. The early morning encounter in the family room. The unexpected (or sometimes expected) surprise awaiting our arrival home from work. House soiling. It is a dirty habit, especially considering the size of the German Shorthair. In many of these cases, the problem had an origin traceable to puppyhood; for others, it results from developmental behavioral and/or health problems. Regardless of the cause, you can take an active role in most cases to minimize or stop completely this annoying habit.

Don't expect to break your dog of this nasty habit by sticking its face and nose in the excrement after-the-fact. Not only is this action illogical, some

Separation anxiety can occur when a Shorthair is separated from its family "pack."

going to be kept in an outdoor enclosure still need to be housetrained as puppies, just in case the need arises later in life to bring them indoors (for whatever reason). If you miss this chance when it is a puppy, you'll be in for trouble later on.

Contrary to popular opinion, you can teach an old dog new tricks, but it takes longer! With older canines that weren't properly housetrained, proceed with training or retraining as you would a puppy. Along with lots of praise, a favorite treat or snack can also be used to reinforce desired behavior. For those times you can't be at home to monitor indoor activity, put the dog into a travel kennel or small bathroom, since dogs are less likely to have premeditated accidents in such confined spaces. Just be reasonable as to the amount of time you make a dog wait between eliminations.

Inappropriate elimination activity can also result from separation anxiety. Dogs left on their own will often become frustrated and soil one or more parts of the house as a result. Some dogs will target furniture, bedding, and, if kept in the garage, even the roofs of automobiles. If it truly is separation anxiety, most of this adverse behavior will occur within 15 to 20 minutes after the owner departs; such predictability can assist in efforts to correct the problem. Treat it as you would any other case of separation anxiety.

The desire to delineate territory is another reason why a dog may choose to urinate (or sometimes defecate) indiscriminately. Certainly, intact male German Shorthaired Pointers are more prone to this instinctive activity. Dogs have such a keen sense of smell that the mere presence of a canine trespasser around the perimeter of the home can set off a urine-marking binge. Owners who move into pre-owned homes often find out the hard way that the previous owners

dogs may even enjoy it! Instead, you need to take a more rational approach to identifying the cause and solving the problem.

Lack of, or improper, housetraining during puppyhood is undoubtedly the most common cause of housesoiling. Many Shorthair owners can't understand why their puppy has no problems going on newspaper, but just can't get the knack of going outside when the newspapers aren't there. They seem to forget that, to a puppy, newspaper and grass are two different surfaces with different smells. To papertrain a puppy, and then expect it to switch easily to another type of surface is asking a lot, and often presents a confusing dilemma to the poor little pup. Puppies need to be taught right from the start to go outside for the elimination process instead of encouraging them to go within the confines of the home. At the same time, German Shorthairs that are

had a poorly trained or highly territorial house dog. Neutering your pet may or may not be helpful, depending upon its age. In many of these older males, it has become more habit than hormonal, and neutering does little to prevent it. Use of a pet odor neutralizer on the carpet and baseboards is warranted if you suspect that a previous occupant is to blame. Use of fencing or dog repellent (not poison!) around the perimeter of the house may also help keep conceited urine-markers away from your house.

An extremely submissive behavior often results in a cowering dog who urinates whenever anyone approaches. This type of adverse elimination is common in dogs that experienced adverse socialization as puppies or spent most of their growing years in a kennel or pound facility. Management of such behavior focuses upon your actions and body language when approaching or greeting such a dog. Try to avoid direct eye contact and sudden physical contact, for by doing so, you can send the dog into immediate submissiveness. If you've been gone from the house for awhile, avoid sudden and exuberant greetings when you get home. By ignoring it initially, you'll lower your dog's excitement level, reduce the immediate threat to it, and give it no reason to urinate. One trick you can try is to immediately and casually walk over to your dog's food bowl and place some food or treats in it. The idea is to distract its attention away from the excitement of your arrival, and create a more comfortable, pleasing situation for it. Once you've been home awhile, then you can and should offer more of your attention.

Finally, don't forget that some diseases or illnesses can cause a pet to urinate or defecate indiscriminately. For instance, dogs that tend to defecate inside the house should be checked for internal parasites. Diets increased in their fiber content can also increase the amount of trips your pet will need to take outdoors. Certainly if the stools are semi-formed, or seem to differ from normal appearance or consistency, an underlying medical reason should be suspected. Some of the conditions that can increase the frequency and/or urge to urinate include urinary tract infections, kidney disease, and diabetes mellitus. For this reason, don't just assume that your dog's soiling problem is purely mental. Have the potential medical causes ruled out first, then you can concentrate on behavioral modification.

Just a word about cleaning up an accident in the house. When using cleaners to tackle the initial mess, be sure they don't contain ammonia. Dog urine contains a form of ammonia, and such products may actually attract your dog back to the same spot later on. Along this same line, after the initial manual cleaning, your next job is to ensure that residual smell doesn't attract your pet back to the same spot. To accomplish this, you need to employ a product containing odor neutralizers specifically targeted for dogs. These products are available in grocery stores or your favorite pet supply store. Deodorizers should not be used, for it is virtually impossible to completely mask or hide a scent from the keen canine nose.

Digging

Though separation anxiety can cause digging episodes, on the average, its influence is much less than with other problem behaviors. Instead, sheer boredom and/or instinctive behavior are the two common state-of-minds that compel a dog to dig. Dogs with nothing else to do may opt for yard excavation to just help pass the time or use up extra energy. The urge to break out of confinement and roam the neighborhood can also compel a

Digging is a nuisance behavior that can be caused by sheer boredom.

dog to start digging. Some dogs will dig to create a spot in which to lie and stay cool on a hot day. Finally, as you may have already experienced, many like to bury personal items such as bones or toys only for exhumation at a later date. Such instinctive behavior, though aggravating, can hardly be considered abnormal, and thus is difficult to totally eliminate.

Increasing your dog's daily dose of exercise may be just what the doctor ordered to help resolve its boredom and release any pent-up energy. Diverting the attention of a chronic digger is another plausible treatment approach; for instance, some troublesome cases have responded very well to the addition of another canine playmate. Rawhide bones and other chewing devices can also be used as attention-grabbers, but only if they don't end up underground themselves. If most of the digging occurs at night, overnight confinement to the garage may be the answer to spare your yard from the ravages of claws. Finally, if not already done, neutering can sometimes help snuff out the strong urge to dig in those dogs wanting to roam.

Destructive Chewing

Many canines are literally "in the doghouse" with their owners because of this destructive behavior. No one wants a pet who seeks and destroys any inanimate object it can sink its teeth into. However, the urgency for dealing with such behavior is not just governed by personal property damage. Many of these chewers also end up in veterinary hospitals suffering from gastroenteritis or intestinal obstructions. Hence, such adverse activity can cost more than just replacement value of furniture or fixtures. It can even sometimes cost the life of a pet!

In puppies, destructive chewing can easily arise from lack of training and from inappropriate selection of toys. Although puppies are naturally going to explore their environment with their mouths, they need to learn at an early age what is and isn't acceptable to chew on. Solid command training is a must for such young pups. Avoid providing normal household items such as old shoes, T-shirts, or sweatshirts as toys to play with. Puppies can't tell the difference between an old shoe and a new shoe, and may decide to try out your new pair for a snack one afternoon! Objects that repeatedly bear the brunt of your dog's teeth should obviously be placed as far out of reach as possible. For furniture or immovable objects, special pet repellents should be sprayed around their perimeters to make a mischievous puppy think twice before sinking its teeth into the item.

In young to middle-aged Shorthairs, separation anxiety is probably the number one cause of destructive chewing. In these cases, the destructive behavior results from an owner's departure from the house, even for a few minutes. In these instances, correction of the problem should focus upon correction of the anxiety attack.

Finally, as with problem barking, boredom plays a leading role in the destructive chewing of some adult dogs. If you think this may be the case, increase your dog's daily activity, and provide it with plenty of alternative targets, such as rawhides or nylon bones, on which to chew. Divert its attention, and most likely its chewing will be diverted as well.

Jumping

Talk about annoying behavior; this one is right up there with house soiling and incessant barking. "Jumpers," as we shall call them, are usually right there at the door when visitors call, and have this innate tendency to spoil a perfectly cordial greeting. After all, nobody wants a dog with dirty paws to jump on their nice, clean clothes, especially if the dog weighs fifty pounds or more!

This is one problem behavior that should never be allowed to gain a firm root in a puppy. Probably the best way to assure this is through strict command training, starting at an early age. Until it learns its commands, be sure to discourage it from jumping on you or family members when the occasion arises. When it does jump at or on you, quickly push it off with your hands and shout "No." Or, as an alternative, flex your knee and make sudden, but gentle contact with its chest, making it fall backwards.

For adult dogs who never learned their manners, a refresher course in command training is the most effective method of curing the chronic jumper. Sometimes, dogs that jump may be simply trying to tell their owners that they want more attention. In such cases, a few more moments of your time devoted to your furry friend each day is an important adjunct to therapy.

Fear of Loud Noises/Gun Shyness

Fear induced by loud noises such as thunder or gunshots can be a common cause of aberrant behavior in German Shorthaired Pointers. Many persons may argue that because of the ultra-sensitive hearing of dogs, pain induced by the noise may play a bigger role than fear itself. Regardless of the reason, when confronted with the disturbing sound, these dogs often become hysterical and quite destructive in their attempts to escape. Many may injure themselves or their owners in the process.

For dogs that fear the sound of thunder, fireworks, etc., owners must avoid direct attempts at comforting the pet, since doing so would be indirectly rewarding the undesirable behavior. If your dog is the type that "comes unglued" in these situations, consider letting it "ride out the storm" in its travel kennel. In addition, playing a radio or television loudly in the vicinity of your pet may help muffle some of the fearful sounds, as well as make your friend feel more at ease. Your veterinarian can prescribe anti-anxiety medications for your dog if it has an exceptional fear of these types of loud noises. In any event, these should be used sparingly and only as needed.

Contrary to popular belief, gun nervousness is not an instinctive behavior, but rather a learned one in gun dogs. As a result, steadiness in the presence of gunfire must be taught at an early age and it must be taught properly to prevent a nervous pup. Gun nervousness should be differentiated from actual gun shyness. If a pup is nervous around a gun it will act quite startled when the gun is discharged and may be reluctant to respond to your commands. These dogs may also quickly lose their desire for the hunt, wanting instead to remain meekly at the side of their master. This condition results from an improper introduction to the firearms and the resulting traumatic mental imprint that occurs. Gun shyness, on the other hand, is actually a rare phenomenon, but when it appears it usually spells disaster. Gun shyness is characterized by terrorized reaction to gunfire that sends the dog off into a panicked flight. It is an inherent defect that can be found within select pedigrees. Unfortunately, dogs suffering from true gun shyness rarely make acceptable hunting dogs.

If you suspect that your Shorthair may be truly gun shy, or if your dog remains nervous around the sound of gunfire even after training, consult your veterinarian. He/she will be able to recommend behavior modification therapies that can be employed in an attempt to salvage your Shorthair's usefulness as a hunter. Although success rates in treating true gun shyness are fair to poor, it is worth a chance exploring such treatment options, considering the alternative.

Purchasing a puppy from a reputable breeder will greatly reduce the chances of acquiring a gun shy dog. Also, purchasing a partially trained or fully-trained gun dog that has been properly introduced to firearms will virtually eliminate this chance altogether.

Aggressiveness

Of all of the undesirable behaviors a dog may exhibit, this one is certainly the most disturbing and the most unacceptable. This aggressiveness may be directed toward other dogs, or toward other species, including humans. Certainly dogs harboring an uncontrollable inherent aggressiveness toward the latter pose special problems to their owners in terms of liability as well. Fortunately, aggressiveness is a rare problem in the German Shorthaired Pointer.

Dominance certainly plays an important role in canine aggressiveness. Some dogs refuse to submit to authority and will lash out at anyone or anything that attempts to exert such. In many instances, these dogs were not properly socialized and/or trained when they were young. In others, sex hormones, namely testosterone, may exert a strong influence as well.

Treatment for such aggressiveness consists of a return to basic command and obedience training. In addition, exercises designed to re-establish dominance can be recommended by your veterinarian and should be performed as well. If the aggression is directed toward a particular person in general, he/she too should be included in these exercises. Remember: Extreme caution and a good, strong muzzle are both advised before any attempts at such dominance assertion are made! For domineering male dogs, neutering is recommended prior to any attempts at retraining.

Fear and pain are two other common causes of aggressive showings in canines. If a dog feels threatened or overwhelmingly fearful, it naturally experiences a "fight or flight" syndrome and may choose the former option over the latter, depending upon how it perceives its options. In addition, dogs have been known to naturally lash out in fear at humans or other animals upon being startled or, more frequently, when they are experiencing pain. For this reason, sudden aggressive changes in personality with or without other signs of illness warrant a complete check-up by your veterinarian.

Treating fear-induced aggression is aimed at reducing the threat you or others pose to your pet. If fear aggression is induced by some outside stimulus, such as a gunshot, then proper restraint and isolation is recommended while the stimulus lasts. If a dog suffers from a vision or hearing deficit, attempts should be made to capture the dog's attention prior to approach.

Not only is physical punishment a useless tool for training, it can lead to natural, aggressive backlashes due to pain (and fear). This is just one more reason why such punishment should be avoided.

For those dogs suffering from injuries or illnesses, remember to always approach and handle them with caution, for although they may not mean to, they could exhibit aggressive tendencies due to the pain associated with the disease.

Dogs, male or female, will certainly defend property they deem theirs, and may not hesitate to fight for it. Territorial aggressiveness toward unwelcome animals or people is not uncommon, as any utility meter reader would attest to! Such aggressive behavior can be just as easily sparked by a perceived encroachment while the dog is eating, or while it is playing with its favorite toy. Many bite wounds to owners have been inflicted because of such actions.

A return to the basics of command training with or without neutering should help curb some of the territorial aggressiveness that may be exhibited by some dogs. In those instances where dogs exhibit aggressiveness toward other dogs they deem a threat to their territory, neutering will help in the majority of the cases.

Certainly showing some respect for a dog's "private property" (toys, bowls, etc.) and eating privacy is a common-sense way to avoid this type of aggressive behavior. It is of vital importance to impress this concept upon children, since they can be frequent violators of the rule. If a dog seems particularly possessive over toys, bones, etc., then excessive sources of the problem should be reduced by eliminating all but one or two of the items. Also, consider feeding the dog in an isolated area of the house away from disturbances.

The best treatment for most types of aggression is prevention. By adhering to the principles of proper socialization and by proper command training, most behavioral problems related to aggressiveness can be avoided altogether. However, for any Shorthair exhibiting aggressiveness, a thorough physical examination and consultation with a veterinarian is

Proper obedience training can curb many behavioral problems.

indicated. Ruling out underlying medical causes is certainly one reason for this; the other is that your veterinarian may choose to prescribe medications to assist in retraining efforts or as a direct attempt to curb the psychological aspects of your dog's aggressiveness. Human anti-anxiety medications such as amitriptyline-HCl and diazepam are being used more and more in veterinary medicine as effective replacements for progestin hormonal therapy (which can have many unpleasant side effects) to help assist in the correction of many behavioral problems, including aggressiveness. Ask your veterinarian for more details.

HOW-TO: Housebreaking Your Puppy

Housebreaking puppies should be started at an early age; preferably as close to eight weeks of age as possible. The reason: This is when the period of stable learning begins in adolescent dogs.

Recognize that puppies have four fairly predictable elimination times: (1) after waking, (2) after eating, (3) after exercising, and (4) just before retiring for the night. Make a concerted effort to take your puppy outside during these times, and every three to four hours in between. When you suspect that it has to go, take it outside and set it down in the grass. If it eliminates, praise it like it was going out of style and then take it immediately back inside the house. By doing so, you'll help it associate the act with the location. If a minute passes and your pup hasn't gone, take it back inside. Don't leave it outside to play or roam. Puppies trained in this manner soon realize that their primary business for being outside is to eliminate, not to play.

What happens if you catch your puppy in mid-act? If this is the case, go ahead and rush it outside. It may finish what it started before you make it outside, but don't get upset. Again, praise your puppy immensely, then bring it immediately back inside. If you happen to miss an accident altogether, don't fret. If you saw it happen, a verbal punishment is indicated. However, if you didn't see it happen, DO NOTHING! Simply try to be more attentive next time.

Other Housetraining Tips to Remember

1. Be sure your puppy is current on its vaccines (since it will be going outside), and is free of intestinal parasites. The latter is very important, since the presence of worms in the intestinal tract will cause unpredictable urges to eliminate.

2. Always use lots of praise; never physically punish. Again, remember that puppies crave praise. If they don't get it, they feel punished. As a result, give plenty of praise when they deserve it; hold it back when they don't. Physical punishment will serve no purpose except to make your training more difficult, and possibly to desocialize your puppy at the same time. And don't ever stick a puppy's nose in its eliminations as a form of punishment.

3. When verbal punishment is indicated, avoid associating your puppy's name with the reprimand. For instance, simply say "Bad," instead of "Bad Dog, Chessy." By leaving your dog's name out of it, it won't associate the name with the bad behavior.

4. Establish a regular feeding schedule for your new puppy. Feed no more than twice daily, and take it outside after it finishes each meal. It is preferable to feed the evening portion before 6:00 PM. This will help reduce the number of overnight accidents that may otherwise occur.

5. To help prevent accidents, keep your puppy in a confined area at night. This area should be puppy-proofed, and be floored such that it won't be damaged if a slip-up occurs. Utility rooms and half-bathrooms work well for this purpose. In addition, the kitchen can be cornered off. If an accident occurs during the night or while you are away, don't get upset. As your training sessions progress, you'll find that this will become less and less of a problem. A natural instinct of any canine is to keep its "den" clean. These inherent instincts, combined with correct house training efforts on your part, will help fuel the success of your training efforts.

6. When cleaning up an accident, always use an odor neutralizer instead of a deodorizer on the area in question. These are available at most pet stores, and will in most cases effectively eliminate any lingering scents which may lure your pet back to the same spot. Avoid using ammonia-based cleaners, since ammonia is a normal component of canine urine. Such cleaners might serve to attract, rather than repel, repeat offenders.

Proper training as a puppy can prevent house soiling.

Training Your German Shorthaired Pointer

Proper training is definitely the key to a happy and fulfilling relationship between you and your German Short-haired Pointer. First of all, it establishes your dominance in the relationship between you and your companion right from the start, and can help prevent many behavioral problems before they appear later on. Not only that, solid training can also keep your friend out of troublesome situations that could threaten both its health and yours!

Owning a well-trained gun dog is not only rewarding and fun, but it makes the hunting experience much more pleasurable and productive. Well-trained German Shorthaired Pointers exhibit certain behavioral patterns that set them apart from their peers. Indeed, the sharply responsive hunting dog will stay at its trainer's heel until commanded to do otherwise. In addition, it will stay within the desired hunting range of the trainer and will respond to its command if this range is exceeded. Highly trained Pointers also remain staunch on point in the presence of game and remain so even after the game is flushed and subsequently shot. Only upon a retrieval or a release command does the dog break point. Finally, if commanded to retrieve, it will deliver the dead or injured game to its handler unadulterated.

In contrast to this model of efficiency, a poorly trained hunting dog can indeed put a damper on any hunting trip. Such dogs will negatively affect the production of a day's hunt by flushing birds far ahead of the advancing hunter. There is nothing more frustrating than to hear the sound of game birds taking to flight 50 to 100 yards ahead of you, completely out of gun range, and there is absolutely nothing that you can do about it! You can always identify the owners of poorly trained gun dogs—they are the ones who are hoarse by the end of the day from screaming at their dogs. Not surprisingly, these unruly dogs are profound nuisances to fellow hunters and can quickly lead you to be blacklisted among your hunting clique.

The good news is that this last scenario can be prevented if you are willing to invest the time, effort, patience, and money into molding a highly trained, highly effective field companion. Obedience training, which should be started as early as eight weeks of age, involves the teaching and practice of basic commands that will allow you to control your dog in any given setting. To achieve maximum training results when obedience training, plan on devoting at least 15 minutes twice a day to the task. Schedule one of these training times immediately upon arrival home from work. Your dog will be excited to have you home and will link the training experience to this pleasure of being reunited with its "pack." Another good time to train is very early in the morning. Puppies are very receptive to learning during this time and a good vigorous training

Remaining staunch on point is a characteristic of a disciplined hunter.

session prior to departing for work can also help calm those dogs that might get anxious at seeing you leave.

If you are not planning to use your German Shorthaired Pointer for hunting or competition, obedience training is all it will need. However, if you want a hunter on your hands, then field training will be needed as well to mold and enhance certain behaviors and hunting patterns in your dog.

Two keys to effective training are consistency and repetition.

Between the ages of two and four months, your puppy should be introduced to the field. Between four and nine months of age, its pointing and retrieving abilities should be refined and firearm conditioning begun. Finally, between nine and fourteen months of age, advanced field-training techniques, such as honoring another dog's point and remaining steady to wing and shot, can be taught. Your ultimate goal is to have a trained dog in the field soon after its first birthday. Don't make the mistake of expecting perfection from your dog during its first few seasons. Instead, the hands-on experience will serve as a further training tool to refine your dog's skills. Perfection will come with practice, and patience and diligence on your part will be rewarded.

Ideally, field-training sessions should be held at least two times a week. For German Shorthaired Pointer puppies under four months of age, hold your training to a maximum of twenty minutes per session. Every week or so add five minutes to the training session, working up to a maximum of 60 minutes for dogs under eight months of age. Also, space out your training sessions as evenly as possible during the week. For instance, holding one session on a Wednesday and the other on a Saturday or Sunday is better than holding both sessions on Saturday and/or Sunday.

The magic success formula for all training endeavors, be they for obedience or for field performance, is derived from two key concepts: consistency and repetition. Consistency provides the building blocks; repetition is the mortar that holds the program together. Without the two, your training efforts will be futile. Consistency means more than just using the same commands over and over again. It also means using the same praises and corrections each time, and keeping your voice tones and/or whistle commands consistently unique for each. Even your body language and postures used during training should remain uniform between sessions. As trivial as it may seem, your Pointer will pick up on stuff like that. Dogs like routine, so stick to it. Train at the same hour each day, and for the same length of time for each daily session. Just as important as consistency to a dog's learning process is repetition. Repeating an action or training drill over and over will help reinforce the positive response you are looking for. Furthermore, the more repetition you implement into training, the leaner and more refined your dog's learned skills become.

Use verbal praise instead of physical pain in your training sessions. Dogs, especially puppies, should always be rewarded for a job well done with lots of praise and attention on your part. Food treats are fine as a reward supplement, but they should never replace verbal compliments.

Punishment may be indicated if your puppy or dog purposely disobeys a command or commits an undesirable act. Yet this should never take the form of physical punishment. There are alternative means, each of which is at least as effective as physical violence. Dogs can be reprimanded effectively with a sharp verbal "No," or by banishment into confinement. Water sprayers, air horns, a can full of coins, hand-held vacuums, etc. can all be used to quickly gain your dog's attention without inflicting any pain.

If used, institute the punishment quickly, preferably within five seconds of the act. If you don't apply it before this time expires, any punishment thereafter may serve to satisfy your anger, but will serve no useful training purpose. Don't extend your punishment past a few seconds. Prolonged exhortations will only confuse your dog and cause you to lose your voice.

Always praise your Pointer for a job well done.

Never use your dog's name during the negative reinforcement. If you do, it may start to associate its name with the bad act and eventually become a basket case whenever its name is called. Reserve this name calling for positive, happy experiences only.

If you do punish, always follow it up shortly thereafter with a command or drill that will lead to a praise situation. Always end your time together on a positive note, and you'll make progress in leaps and bounds.

Training Equipment

Equipment you will need for obedience training your German Shorthaired Pointer includes a chain-training collar, a six-foot leather or web lead, a 32-foot retractable lead (or nylon check cord), two whistles, and a travel kennel. In addition, for advanced field training, you'll need a .22 caliber blank pistol,

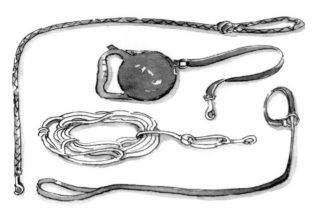

Various types of leads and check cords.

Table 7: Training Equipment
- Chain Training Collar (Choke Collar)
- 32-Foot Retractable Lead/Check Cord
- Training Whistles
- Travel Kennel
- .22 Caliber Blank Pistol
- Retrieving Lure
- Release Cages
- Live Game

a retrieving lure, live game, and release cages. Your local hunting and gun clubs can help direct you to sources of these latter two items.

A chain-training collar, commonly referred to as a "choke" collar, is an invaluable training tool. This collar does not actually choke a dog when properly applied, but rather it is designed to exert quick and temporary pressure at the dog's neck region, promoting submission. When applied, the collar should be large enough so that you can comfortably fit two fingers between the collar and the neck with minimal pressure felt on the fingers. Remember, for maximum effectiveness and

A blank pistol is an essential tool for field training.

safety, this type of collar should be worn only during training sessions.

Just a quick word about electronic training devices and collars. These devices are generally not required for training German Shorthaired Pointers if proper obedience commands are taught at an early age. However, for the unruly student or one that is slow to respond to obedience or field training, electronic training devices may be useful. Be sure to follow the instructions contained within the unit carefully or, better yet, consult your veterinarian on the proper use of these devices.

The six-foot leather lead and 32-foot retractable lead or check cord will come in handy for teaching basic obedience commands and the latter for controlling range during field training. Leads can be purchased at any pet store or discount store. These items are also available through mail-order catalogs.

Another item you'll want to put on your shopping list is a training whistle. Consider using a whistle instead of your voice to train your dog, for it allows for consistent commands every time (not to mention it will save your voice). Just remember to always carry a spare with you to the field in case your primary whistle malfunctions. The type of whistle you use is simply a matter of personal preference; however, avoid using silent whistles. Also, if you ever have to replace a whistle, make certain the new whistle you purchase is similar in sound and pitch to the one you use to train your dog initially.

A travel kennel will be needed to transport your dog to and from the field. Be sure the one you get is large enough for it to turn around in, yet small enough to prevent unnecessary movement during transport.

Two other pieces of equipment you'll want to obtain if you are planning to use your German Shorthaired Pointer for hunting include a .22 caliber blank pistol and a retrieving lure. The .22 caliber pistol will be needed to begin conditioning your pup to the sound of gunfire. These pistols are relatively inexpensive and can be obtained through gunshops, sporting goods stores, and even mail-order catalogs. Also, if you are going to teach your shorthair to retrieve, you'll need a retrieving lure. They can be obtained commercially or you can make one at home using a sock, reinforced tape, and some feathers from an upland game bird. The texture and firmness of the lure should mimic that of an upland game bird. A lure that is too hard and solid may promote rough handling ("hard mouth") by your dog, as it must grip it tightly in order to hold on to it.

Obedience Training

The essential obedience commands you will want to teach your Shorthair include whoa, release, come-in, heel, sit, down, and kennel. Although other more specialized commands do exist for those dogs going on to compete in obedience trials, these seven are the ones that you will find most useful at home and in the field. German Shorthaired Pointers are quite intelligent and most puppies will pick up these commands quite easily.

Whoa

The most important obedience command your Shorthair needs to

Release cages for live game.

learn is the command to stop, or "whoa." This command tells your dog to stop immediately and stand at attention. In the field, the "whoa" command will be used to control your dog's range and to keep it staunch when it goes on point. "Whoa" is also useful for keeping a dog steady to wing and shot, and for reinforcing a dog that is honoring the point of another. Finally, it is an indispensable tool for keeping your dog out of harm's way both at home and while hunting. In fact, never let your puppy run free of its leash or a check cord until this command is fully mastered.

Begin teaching this command by taking your pup for a walk with a flexible lead attached to its chain training collar. As it begins to distance itself from

A properly applied choke collar for the dog heeling on the trainer's left-hand side.

"Whoa" should be the first command your Shorthair learns.

A sharp tug on a lead and a verbal or whistle command are used to teach a dog to "whoa."

you on the extended lead, catch its attention with a verbal "whoa," followed by one long blast on the whistle, and a firm tug or jerk on the lead. If it stops, walk up to it slowly, repeating the command "whoa" as you approach. Readjust its position if you see fit to do so, then praise it profusely for a job well done. If your dog doesn't stop on the initial command or if it begins to move when you approach it, repeat the whistle blast, verbal command, and sharp tug on the lead until it complies with your wishes.

Once your dog is stationary, start to slowly walk away, extending the flexible lead out by hand. If your dog moves, immediately command it to "whoa" and walk back to it, repeating the command and praising it if it responds to it. Gradually increase the distance you walk away from your dog with each successive training session until you've finally reached the maximum distance on the leash. Only when you feel your Shorthair has mastered this command should you remove the leash from its collar. Even then, do so within the confines of a restricted area such as a fenced yard, just in case your ambitious pup has a sudden lapse of memory!

Release

Release is a go-ahead command for your dog to begin or resume its activities. With your puppy on its check cord, command it to "whoa," immediately followed by one long blast on the whistle. Allow your shorthair to remain in this standing position for 20 to 30 seconds, then say "release," immediately followed by two short blasts on your whistle. After giving the command, enthusiastically begin to walk forward and encourage your puppy to follow you with a firm forward tug on the leash. Avoid the desire to say "come-in" or "heel" to your puppy if it fails to move. Instead, simply walk back to it, repeat the command sequence and guide it forward with your hand on its rear end if necessary.

Come-in

Begin teaching your German Short-haired Pointer to come to you by first stopping your dog using the "whoa" command. Now walk ten feet away from your dog, again manually extending the flexible lead or check cord as you go. Turn and face your dog, kneel down, and say "come-in," followed by three short blasts on your whistle. Most puppies won't hesitate to rush into their trainer's arms. When yours does so, heap on the praise. If it is reluctant to come to you, gently apply pressure toward you with its lead, repeating the command as you do so. One word of caution: Never use this command to call in your dog for punishment. To do so will only serve to confuse your young friend and may actually hinder other training efforts as well.

Heel

An important command you will teach your four-legged student is to "heel" (walk at your side). To begin, position yourself on your Pointer's left-hand side facing forward, with its shoulders even with your knee. Now, in simultaneous fashion, give a quick forward tug on the lead, say "heel," and start forward with your left foot leading. As your dog follows, keep its head level and in control using the leash. Start out by going five yards at a time, then stopping (use your "whoa" command) to praise for a job well done.

If your dog refuses to move on your initial command, go back to the starting line and set up again. This time, if needed, follow the quick tug with an encouraging push forward from the rear end to initiate movement. Start and stop frequently, praising as you go. As your dog starts to catch on, increase the distances you go each

The "come-in" command will prove especially useful during retrieval training.

time. The ultimate goal is to have it walk briskly by your side until a command is given to do otherwise. If it gets too far out in front of you, a sharp, backward tug on the lead should be used to correct the discrepancy. For

Teaching your dog to "come-in."

When at heel, your dog's shoulder should remain even with your knee.

those trainees more interested in playing than learning, stop the training session temporarily and ignore or confine your trainee until it settles down. Don't scold it or show any other acknowledgment of its antics. It will soon learn that you mean business!

Once your dog has become comfortable walking in straight lines by your side, take it through some turns both to the right and to the left. During the turns, your dog's shoulder should remain aligned with your knee.

Sit and Down

"Sit" and "down" are two commands you'll want your dog to learn if it is to compete in obedience trials and dog shows. For the hunter, these two commands are not as vital, yet it certainly won't hurt your dog to learn them.

To teach your Shorthair to sit, start with the "whoa" command to stop your student. Next, pull upward on your dog's lead, say the word "sit," and push down on its rear end to encourage it to sit. Have your dog maintain this posture for a good five seconds, then break into a heel. Gradually increase the amount of time it stays in the sitting position as your training progresses.

The "down" command can be taught after your dog has mastered the "sit" command. Have your dog assume the sitting position, then say the command "down" while applying downward pressure with your free hand to your dog's shoulder region. Note the difference from the "sit" command, in which downward pressure is applied to the hind end. Once your dog has assumed the correct position, command it to "whoa" and begin to slowly walk away. If your dog begins to break position, say "whoa" once more, and if necessary, walk back to your dog and reposition it in the "down" position. Repeat the drill over several training sessions until your dog exhibits a consistent satisfactory response.

Kennel

When you say the word "kennel" to your dog, it should immediately head for its travel carrier or doghouse. To teach your dog this command, attach the retractable lead to its collar, then position your dog approximately ten feet away from its travel carrier, and use the "whoa" command. Now, using "whoa" to keep your dog in place, walk over to the carrier, open the gate, and with your arm pointing toward the entrance, use the command "kennel." If your pupil doesn't move, simply use the lead to reel it in to you and direct it into the kennel. Once your dog goes into the kennel, close the gate behind it and praise. To gain maximum benefit from the word association, allow your Shorthair to remain inside the kennel for a good two minutes prior to releasing. Keep repeating this process until the desired results are achieved without further physical intervention on your part.

Field Training

As mentioned earlier, if you are planning to use your German Shorthaired Pointer for hunting, you'll want to introduce it to the field at a young age. Obviously, to do this, you need to locate a field, preferably one containing game birds. Finding a place to run your pup can be challenging, especially if you live in a city or a suburb. However, there are certain sources to which you can look to find open space in order to train your Shorthair. The first resources to tap are friends and family who may themselves own land or may be able to refer you to landowners who live fairly close by. Don't be afraid to hop in a car and drive thirty miles in order to find a field. The investment in time and gas will pay off in dividends during hunting season. Another way to find a field is to approach local landowners directly. You'll be surprised; most will be more than happy to honor your request, especially if you offer to pay a small fee for the privilege of using their land. You can also contact your state's fish and wildlife agency for locations of public lands that may be available for such training purposes. Be sure to state your purpose clearly to them, as many public areas prohibit dogs on the premises. Also, inquire at local dog clubs, hunting clubs, and shooting preserves concerning leased land that is available to members. Joining such a hunting organization will not only allow you to gain access to fields containing game, but it will also allow you to network with fellow hunters and other owners of German Shorthaired Pointers. Finally, contact your local sporting good outlets and gun shops for leads and locations of potential training sites. They can often provide you with valuable tips and leads to help you accomplish your mission.

Once you've found a field for your Shorthair puppy, introduce the young hunter to it by allowing the pup to run free and chase any game that it may encounter. The purpose for doing so is to stimulate and develop its instinctive hunting behaviors, including finding and pointing game. Whenever your Shorthair goes on point or performs any desirable action, be sure to praise it profusely for doing so, and it will link the pleasure to the act.

Firearm Conditioning

When your puppy reaches four to six months of age, you should begin conditioning it to the sound of gunfire. One effective way to get your shorthair pup used to firearms is to take your .22 caliber blank pistol with you to the field. Let your dog range 20 to 30 yards ahead of you, position the pistol behind your back and fire a shot, noting your dog's reaction. More than likely the sound will startle it and create a glance back in your direction. Act as though nothing has happened and soon your eager hunter will forget about it and move on. Repeat the action again 15 minutes later, and continue to do so at frequent intervals throughout the day. During subsequent sessions, gradually decrease the distance between you and your dog prior to discharging the pistol. Eventually, after seven to ten training sessions, you should be able to fire the pistol within five feet of your dog without causing alarm.

Once your Shorthair becomes accustomed to the sound of a .22 caliber blank pistol, graduate up to a shotgun. As with the initial training, begin at a distance, then gradually decrease the range between you and your dog over subsequent training sessions. When firing the shotgun in the dog's presence, aim high in the air and shoot in the direction of the dog. Again, if your dog appears startled,

The texture and firmness of a training lure should mimic that of an upland game bird.

Honoring a point.

back at you, act as though nothing has happened. Soon, its attention will go back to the lure. With continued conditioning, your dog will soon learn to interpret the sound of gunfire as a "get-ready" signal to retrieve.

One final note: To further solidify your dog's acceptance of gunfire, plan on hunting solo during your dog's first season, and try to limit your shots at game to one. Rookie dogs that are led out into the field and exposed to a barrage of gunfire from a group of overzealous hunters can easily become startled and refuse to hunt.

Staunchness on Point

Pointing out game is a strong natural instinct in your German Shorthaired Pointer, but remaining staunch on that point may not be. Remaining staunch on point means that your dog will hold a tight point until released by you. Teaching a dog to remain staunch on point greatly increases the pleasure of the hunting experience, affording you greater control and giving you time to walk up on the identified game and position yourself for the shot before it is flushed.

There are three types of points that your German Shorthaired Pointer will perform. The first is called a productive point. This is a point in which actual game has been located and is being held by your dog. Certainly, in these cases, staunchness is very important. The second type of point is an unproductive point, in which residual scents left by game that has recently left the area are so strong that it fools the dog into thinking that the game is still there. The third and final type of point is the false point, usually caused by a weak air scent or an old, diluted foot scent. As your dog is moving back and forth through a field or woods it may detect this faint scent and stop for a moment and appear to be on point. In most

act as though nothing has happened. By repeating this procedure over several weeks, your dog won't even bat an eye when a gun is discharged.

Firearm training can also be combined with retrieval training. Have a partner entice your dog with a lure, then throw it high into the air in front of your dog. When your dog's attention turns to the lure, discharge your gun. Again, if your dog stops and stares

instances, such encounters do not result in a staunch point, as the dog soon realizes what has happened and continues the hunt.

To teach your Shorthair to remain staunch on point, you'll need live game. The most popular types of birds used for this type of training are either pigeons or quail. These birds can be placed in small release cages that can be manually or electronically opened to release the game as desired.

To begin this training, strategically place your release cages containing the birds in a field or wooded area (German Shorthaired Pointers are smart; be sure your dog isn't watching you do this!). Next, keeping your dog on its retractable lead or check cord, face it into the wind and slowly approach the release cages. As your dog nears the cages, it will pick up the scent of the birds and should instinctively go on point. When it does, say "whoa," grab hold of its collar to keep it in position, and administer praise. Still maintaining a grip on the collar, adjust your dog's conformation as needed. Tighten the point by pushing your dog's rear end gently in the direction of the bird. As you do, it will instinctively plant its feet firmly and tighten its conformation. If your dog begins to break point, shout "whoa" and return it to its position. Repeat this process over several training sessions until you are satisfied enough with your dog's ability to staunchly hold a point.

Steadiness to Wing and Shot

Dogs that are taught to remain steady to wing and shot will maintain their station even after the game is flushed, moving only when released by the hunter to retrieve the game or to resume hunting. Teaching your dog this skill will prevent it from blindly running after game and potentially flushing out other birds in the immediate area in the process. Again, it

A retractable lead is a useful training aid.

allows you greater control over your hunting companion and increases the productivity of your hunt. Many experts believe that steadiness to wing and shot is the sign of only the most highly polished and trained of gun dogs.

To teach steadiness, lead your dog through the same process as described for teaching staunchness

Proper firearm conditioning will help prevent gun nervousness in hunting dogs.

Teaching staunchness on point.

on point, but this time, you'll want to release the birds from their cages or have an assistant throw one of the birds into the air once your dog has tightened its point. Be sure you have a firm grip on your dog's collar and use the command "whoa" when the birds are flushed. If your dog attempts to break point, command "whoa" again and tug it back in place. Be patient with your Shorthair, as this is an exciting time for it. Repeat this process through several training sessions, removing the lead or check cord as your friend becomes more proficient. Soon, you'll have a hunter that won't budge even when taunted by the most arrogant winged foe!

To teach steadiness to shot, repeat the above sequence, yet this time fire off your .22 caliber blank pistol when the birds take to flight. If your Shorthair breaks point, use the check cord and the "whoa" command to return it to position. As your Pointer becomes proficient over time, graduate up to a shotgun. Repeat the training sequence over and over until you are able to remove the lead or check cord and fire your gun without your dog bolting.

Retrieval Training

Retrieving fallen game is natural for many German Shorthaired Pointers; however, remember that this is not the breed's primary instinct. There are three types of retrievals you can ask your dog to perform. The first is retrieving birds that are shot off of a point. The second is retrieving game that has been shot down in what is called a "hunt dead." This type of retrieve occurs when a dog is brought into a defined area in order to scent and find fallen game that could not otherwise be located. The third type of retrieve, called nonslip retrieving, is called upon when hunting waterfowl and dove. Here, your dog remains at your heel or in your blind until game is shot, then is sent to retrieve it either on land or in water.

One aspect of retrieval training is to teach your dog to have a "soft mouth," that is, to retrieve game tenderly to your hand. It does no good to have your Shorthair retrieve game if it returns it to you in a mutilated condition. Keep in mind that it is instinctive for dogs to handle roughly game that is wounded and struggling. As a result, use a lure versus live game during retrieval training to prevent this instinctive reaction. Be sure to teach and praise your dog for a soft mouth early in its life and never play tug of war with your German Shorthaired Pointer puppy. Although this may seem part of the fun of puppyhood, it only encourages a "hard-mouthed" hunter.

Training your dog to retrieve properly involves more than just throwing a lure off into the distance and having your dog go get it. For maximum results, this exercise should be performed in the field with an assistant and a gun. To start, command your Shorthair to heel at your side and attach a lead or check cord to its collar. Next, have your assistant, who is standing next to you, throw the lure high in the air ten yards out in front. When the lure is released, fire your gun into the air. Wait at least ten seconds after the lure has hit the ground, then give the retrieve command and motion to the fallen game. If necessary, lead your dog to the fallen lure and place it in its mouth. Command your dog to "whoa" and walk back to your original position.

Now command your Shorthair to "come-in" verbally or with three short blasts on the whistle. If it does not respond immediately, give a firm tug on the check cord to remind it who is in control. When your dog gets within ten feet of you, command it to "heel" at your side. Reach down and remove the lure from its mouth and praise for a job well done. If your student is overly rough with the lure or won't let go of it, give a verbal reprimand and manually open its mouth to release the lure.

As with teaching other commands, repeat the process over and over (over several training sessions) until your dog has mastered it.

Honoring a Point

Teaching your dog to honor another hunting dog's point should be considered if you plan on going to the field with fellow hunters who may have dogs of their own hunting with them. When a dog honors another's point, it refrains from rushing in to supplant the dog that originally located and pointed the game. It is the ultimate in hunting dog etiquette!

To train your dog to honor another's point, you'll obviously need a friend

Retrieving doesn't always come naturally to the German Shorthaired Pointer; as a result, retrieval drills should be a part of your dog's overall training.

with an experienced gun dog to assist in the training. To begin, plant a release cage containing a game bird in a field or wooded area and let the other experienced dog find the bird and go on point. Next, with your dog on a lead, bring it up to within ten feet of the other dog. As your dog nears, it should instinctively go on point. If it doesn't, use the command "whoa" to stop it. Have your friend release the bird from its cage. Keep your dog steady with a firm grip on its collar and don't allow it to break. Talk to your dog gently, reinforcing with the "whoa" command if necessary. Release your Shorthair only after the other dog has been released. By repeating this sequence enough times, your dog will soon learn that oft-quoted rule of life, "finder's keepers!"

The Thrill of Competition

The calendar months between hunting seasons need not be filled with idleness and boredom. Instead, consider entering your Shorthair in one of the many AKC and FDSB (Field Dog Stud Book) licensed events occurring throughout the county. Competitive events held under American Kennel Club rules include dog shows, field trials, and obedience trials. There are two types of events within these categories in which you may enter your dog. The first are formal or licensed events in which points are earned toward championship titles. To win a title will not only give you a sense of satisfaction, but it will also make your German Shorthaired Pointer much more valuable for breeding purposes. The second type of event is called a match trial, in which no points are earned. These trials, in which dogs compete for fun for ribbons and trophies, are usually put on by local breed clubs and all-breed obedience clubs. Match trials are a great place to start the aspiring show dog and competitor.

Before entering your dog into any event, make plans to attend several trials as a spectator in order to gain a better understanding of that particular event's procedures and rules. Make the most of your time by mingling with fellow spectators and contestants, asking questions liberally. In fact, it is a good idea to write your questions down prior to attending the event to be sure you come away with a full database! Also, be sure to ask for recommendations pertaining to any books, literature, publications, Internet addresses, electronic mailboxes, and/or chat rooms that could serve to enhance further your knowledge on the subject. Obviously, the more information you can amass prior to your dog becoming an actual contestant, the better are the chances for success for you and your dog when your time comes to compete.

Locations of events in your area can be traced through your local breeders, veterinarians, trainers, dog clubs, and hunt clubs. You can also contact the AKC and FDSB directly for listings of competitions in your locale. A wealth of information can also be searched and retrieved via the Internet concerning competitions for your German Shorthaired Pointer (see page 100).

The thrill of competition.

Dog Shows

The purpose of the dog show is to judge how closely a dog comes to the ideal standard for conformation and physical characteristics for its particular breed. In order for your Shorthair to compete in a dog show, it must not have been spayed or neutered and must not have any breed disqualifications.

There are two types of dog shows. The first, called a specialty show, involves one breed only and is usually put on by the breed's national parent club or local regional club. The second type of dog show is the all-breed show in which multiple breeds compete together. Specialty shows and all-breed shows are often held in conjunction with one another. The judging in these shows is based on the process of elimination, with the eventual winner being crowned Best of Breed or Best of Show.

To be considered an AKC Champion of Record, a dog must amass 15 points by competing in formal licensed events. To impart fairness in scoring, a portion of these 15 points must be won as major point wins under different judges. Each licensed event held will have a designated number of points available for winning, usually from one to five points. This number of points is based upon the number of entrants and region of the country. Dogs compete in one of six classes, including Puppy (6 to 9 Month), Puppy (9 to 12 Month), Novice, Bred-by-Exhibitor, American-bred, and/or Open Class. The winner of a particular class will then go up against the winners in the other five classes to determine which one will be crowned the Winners Dog or the Winners Bitch. These two dogs will then compete with each other for Best of Breed, and this winner, along with the winners representing the various AKC dog groupings, will then compete for the prestigious title of Best in Show.

Dog shows judge how closely an entrant conforms to its breed standards.

In all-breed dog shows, multiple breeds compete together.

Table 8: American Kennel Club Titles

AFC	Amateur Field Champion
CH	Champion
DC	Dual Champion
FC	Field Champion
NAFC	National Amateur Field Champion
NFC	National Field Champion
OTCH	Obedience Trial Champion
TRI-CH	Triple Champion
CD	Companion Dog
CDX	Companion Dog Excellent
JH	Junior Hunter
MH	Master Hunter
SH	Senior Hunter
TD	Tracking Dog
TDX	Tracking Dog Excellent
VST	Variable Surface Tracking
CT	Champion Tracker
UD	Utility Dog
UDT	Utility Dog Tracker
UDTX	Utility Dog Tracker Excellent
NA	Novice Agility
OA	Open Agility
AX	Agility Excellent
MX	Master Agility Excellent

Breed Standards

The following are the standards for the German Shorthaired Pointer that were officially adopted in 1975 by the American Kennel Club. When your Shorthair competes in a dog show, these are the standards it is up against!

The Official AKC Standard for the German Shorthaired Pointer

The Shorthair is a versatile hunter, an all-purpose gun dog capable of high performance in field and water. The judgment of Shorthairs in the show ring should reflect this basic characteristic.

General Appearance—The overall picture which is created in the observer's eye is that of an aristocratic, well-balanced, symmetrical animal with conformation indicating power, endurance and agility and a look of intelligence and animation. The dog is neither unduly small nor conspicuously large. It gives the impression of medium size, but is like the proper hunter, "with a short back, but standing over plenty of ground."

Tall leggy dogs, or dogs which are ponderous or unbalanced because of excess substance should be definitely rejected. The first impression is that of a keenness which denotes full enthusiasm for work without indication of nervous or flighty character. Movements are alertly coordinated without waste motion. Grace of outline, clean-cut head, sloping shoulders, deep chest, powerful back, strong quarters, good bone composition, adequate muscle, well-carried tail and taut coat, all combine to produce a look of nobility and an indication of anatomical structure essential to correct gait which must indicate a heritage of purposefully conducted breeding. Doggy bitches and bitchy dogs are to be faulted. A judge must excuse a dog from the ring if it displays extreme shyness or viciousness toward its handler or the judge. Aggressiveness or belligerence toward another dog is not to be considered viciousness toward its handler or the judge. Aggressiveness or belligerence toward another dog is not to be considered viciousness.

Symmetry—Symmetry and field quality are most essential. A dog in hard and lean field condition is not to be penalized; however, overly fat or poorly muscled dogs are to be penalized. A dog well-balanced in all points is preferable to one with outstanding good qualities and defects.

Head—Clean-cut, neither too light nor too heavy, the head should be in proper proportion to the body. The skull is reasonably broad, arched on side and slightly round on top. The scissura (median line between the eyes at the forehead) is not too deep, the occipital bone is not as conspicuous as in the case of the Pointer. The foreface rises gradually from nose to forehead. The rise is more strongly pronounced in the dog than in the bitch as befitting his sex. The chops fall away from the somewhat projecting nose. Lips are full and deep, never flewy. The chops do not fall over too much, but form a proper fold in the angle. The jaw is powerful and the muscles are well developed. The line to the forehead rises gradually and never has a definite stop as that of the Pointer, but rather a stop-effect when viewed from the side, due to the position of the eyebrows. The muzzle is sufficiently long to enable the dog to seize properly and to facilitate his carrying game a long time. A pointed muzzle is not desirable. The entire head never gives the impression of tapering to a point. The depth is in the right proportion to the length, both in the muzzle and in the skull proper. The length of the muzzle should equal the length of the skull. A pointed muzzle is a fault. A dish-faced muzzle is a fault. A definite Pointer stop is a serious fault. Too many wrinkles in the forehead is a fault.

Ears—Ears are broad and set fairly high, lie flat and never hang away from the head. Placement is just above eye level. The ears, when laid in front without being pulled, meet the lip angle. In the case of heavier dogs, the ears are correspondingly longer. Ears too long or fleshy are to be faulted.

Eyes—The eyes are of medium size, full of intelligence and expression, good humored and yet radiating energy, neither protruding nor sunken. The eye is almond shaped, not circular. The eyelids close well. The best color is dark brown. Light yellow (bird of prey) eyes are not desirable and are a fault. Closely set eyes are to be faulted. China or wall eyes are to be disqualified.

Nose—Brown noses, the larger the better, with nostrils well-opened and broad are desirable. Spotted noses are not desirable. A flesh-colored nose disqualifies.

Teeth—The teeth are strong and healthy. The molars intermesh properly. The bite is a true scissors bite. A perfect level bite (without overlapping) is not desirable and must be penalized. An extreme overshot or undershot bite disqualifies.

Neck—The neck should be of proper length to permit the jaws reaching game to be retrieved, sloping downward on beautifully curving lines. The nape is rather muscular, becoming gradually larger toward the shoulders. Moderate hound-like throatiness is permitted.

Chest—The chest in general gives the impression of depth rather than breadth; for all that, it should be in correct proportion to the other parts of the body with a fair depth. The chest reaches down to the elbows, the ribs forming the thorax show a rib spring and are not flat or slabsided; they are not perfectly round or barrel-shaped. Ribs that are entirely round prevent the necessary expansion of the chest when taking breath. The back ribs reach well down. The circumference of the thorax immediately behind the elbows is smaller than that of the thorax about a hands-breadth behind elbows, so that the upper arm has room for movement.

Back, Loins, and Croup—Back is short, strong, and straight with slight rise from root of tail to withers. Loin strong, of moderate length and slightly arched. Tuck-up is apparent. Excessively long, roached, or swayed back must be penalized.

Forequarters—The shoulders are sloping, movable, well-covered with muscle. The shoulder blades lie flat and are well laid back, nearing a 45 degree angle. The upper arm (the bones between the shoulder and elbow joints) is as long as possible, standing away somewhat from the trunk so that the straight and closely muscled legs, when viewed from the front, appear to be parallel. Elbows which stand away from the body or are too close indicate toes turning inwards or outwards, which must be regarded as faults. Pasterns are strong, short, and nearly vertical with a slight spring. Loose, short-bladed, or straight shoulders must be faulted. Knuckling over is to be faulted. Down in the pasterns is to be faulted.

Hindquarters—The hips are broad with hip sockets wide apart and fall slightly toward the tail in a graceful curve. Thighs are strong and well-muscled. Stifles bend well. Hock joints are well angulated with strong, straight bone structure from hock to pad. Angulation of both stifle and hock joint is such as to combine maximum combination of both drive and traction. Hocks turn neither in nor out. A steep croup is a fault. Cowhocked legs are a serious fault.

Feet—The feet are compact, close-knit, and round to spoon-shaped. The toes are sufficiently arched and heavily nailed. The pads are strong, hard, and thick. Dewclaws on the forelegs may be removed. Feet pointing in or out is a fault.

Coat and Skin—The skin is close and tight. The hair is short and thick and feels tough to the hand; it is somewhat longer on the underside of the tail and the back edges of the haunches. It is softer, thinner, and shorter on the ears and the head. Any dog with long hair in body coat is to be severely penalized.

Tail—The tail is set high and firm, and must be docked, leaving 40 percent of its length. The tail hangs down when the dog is quiet, and is held horizontally when he is walking. The tail must never be curved over the back toward the head when the dog is moving. A tail curved or bent toward the head is to be severely penalized.

Bones—Thin and fine bones are by no means desirable in a dog which must possess strength and be able to work over any and every countryside. The main importance is not laid so much on the size of bone, but rather on their being in proper proportion to the body. Bone structure too heavy or too light is a fault. Dogs with coarse bones are handicapped in agility of movement and speed.

Weight and Height—The weight of dogs should be 55 to 70 pounds. Bitches should weigh 45 to 60 pounds. Dogs should measure 23 to 25 inches. Bitches should measure 21 to 23 inches at the withers. Deviations of one inch above or below the described heights are to be severely penalized.

Color—The coat may be of solid liver or any combination of liver and white, such as liver and white ticked, liver spotted and white ticked, or liver roan. A dog with any area of black, red, orange, lemon, or tan, or a dog that is solid white will be disqualified.

Gait—A smooth, lithe gait is essential. It is to be noted that as gait increases from the walk to a faster speed, the legs converge beneath the body. The tendency to single track is desirable. The forelegs reach well ahead as if to pull in the ground without giving the appearance of a hackney gait, and are followed by the back legs which give forceful propulsion. Dragging the rear feet is undesirable.

Disqualifications

China or wall eyes.

Flesh-colored nose.

Extreme overshot or undershot.

A dog with any area of black, red, orange, lemon, or tan, or a solid white dog.

(Reprinted with Kind Permission from the American Kennel Club)

Obedience Trials

The second type of competition you can enter your German Shorthaired Pointer into is the obedience trial. In obedience trials, dogs are put through a defined group of exercises and commands, with their performance scored by a judge. Obedience trial scores are not dependent upon conformation or other breed standards. In fact, dogs that have been neutered or have other physical defects are welcome to compete in these events.

There are multiple levels or titles that dogs compete for in obedience trials. These include competitions for Novice/Companion Dog (CD), Open/Companion Dog Excellent (CDX), and Utility/Utility Dog (UD) and Utility Dog Excellent (UDX). Each dog-handler team starts out with a perfect score of 200, and points are then deducted for slowness, lack of attention, and/or vocalization. In fact, if a handler must repeat a command, the team is automatically disqualified. In order to win a title, a team must end up with at least 170 points under three different judges on three different days.

In the Novice competition, dogs perform six obedience exercises, which include Heel on Leash, Stand for Examination, Heel off Leash, Recall (come when called), Long Sit (one minute), and Long Down (three minutes). Dogs that accumulate enough points competing in the various shows can earn the title Companion Dog (CD). Once a dog has earned its Companion Dog degree, it can then

Obedience trials test a dog's responsiveness to commands.

compete in the open competition. In this event, there are seven exercises that dogs are put through. These include Heel Free, Drop on Recall, Retrieve on Flat, Retrieve Over High Jump, Broad Jump, Long Sit (three minutes), and Long Down (five minutes). After a dog has qualified in three shows and has earned enough points, it can then receive its CDX title. Only after this title is awarded can the contestant advance on to the utility competition. This includes a signal exercise such as heeling upon a hand signal, two scent discrimination tests, directed retrieve, directed jumping over hurdles, and finally, group examination. Title winners in this competition are then allowed to compete

93

for the obedience trial championship and the title of Obedience Trial Champion.

In addition to the above trials, there are two tracking levels of titles in which dogs may compete. In these tracking tests, dogs are required to follow scents that have been aged over a specified distance. The tracking titles that can be won include Tracking Dog (TD), Tracking Dog Excellent (TDX), and Variable Surface Tracking (VST). Once a dog earns all three titles, it is considered a Champion Tracker (CT).

Agility Competitions

A newer type of competitive event that has become quite popular is the agility competition. In these events, dogs are guided by their owners over a course filled with, among other things, obstacles they must jump over, tires and tunnels they must go through, and poles they must weave in and out of. These are timed events, measuring agility under pressure. Penalties are assessed if obstacles are missed or knocked down, or if time runs out before the course is finished. As with other types of competitive events, various levels of proficiency receive awards, from the most basic to the most advanced agility talents. Titles awarded include Novice Agility (NA), Open Agility (OA), Agility Excellent (AX), and Master Agility Excellent (MX). At each level, a dog must pass the agility test three times under two different judges before it can earn a title and advance to the next level. Dogs that earn the coveted MX title are the agile elite! In order for one to earn this degree, it must pass the AX level test no less than ten times!

Field Trials

For the serious enthusiast, field trials offer a chance to extend the thrill of the hunt beyond bird season. They also provide an excellent venue for honing hunting skills and maintaining a bird dog in top condition. Field trials are designed to test the ability of a dog to perform the original functions of the breed in which it is a member. German Shorthaired Pointers compete in field trials designated for the pointing breeds. These trials include exercises which test the ability of the dog to scent out game, to go on point, and to remain staunch on that point.

Over a thousand of these competitive events are held throughout the United States each year. Most are conducted on weekends, held by clubs operating under either AKC or FDSB rules. A single field trial actually consists of a number of competitions, or stakes. Individual stakes are characterized by certain restrictions and rules designed to maintain a competitive fairness. Qualifications for individual stakes take into account the experience of the handler, the method of transportation used in the stake (i.e. horseback vs. walking on foot), the age of the dog, and the dog's past accomplishments. Each dog and/or handler is allowed to enter all stakes for which he/she meets the imposed restrictions.

Various courses are designed to simulate natural hunting conditions and scenarios. Competing dogs hunt planted game such as quail and pheasant. During each stake, dogs are run in pairs (braces), with the handlers following behind on horseback or on foot. The judges and trial marshall generally follow all the action on horseback.

AKC Field Trials

AKC field trials consist of member trials, which are held by AKC member clubs, and licensed trials, which are put on by nonmember clubs. Most AKC field trials are not restricted to a single breed, but rather are open to all pointing breeds recognized by the AKC. Within these local trials, dogs compete for the title of Field Champion or Amateur Field Champion. Those dogs awarded these titles in the local competitions can go on to compete for the coveted National Field Champion and National Amateur Field Champion Titles at the National Championship Field Trials sponsored by the national breed club.

FDSB Field Trials

The majority of FDSB Field Trials held are nontitle events called feeder trials. Dogs that place in these feeder trials can then compete for titles in the larger FDSB championship trials. Among the organizations that conduct field trials falling under FDSB guidelines are the National Shoot-to-Retrieve Association (NSTRA), the National Bird Hunters Association (NBHA), the American Bird Hunters Association (ABHA), and the United States Complete Shooting Dog Association (USCSDA). If interested, contact the FDSB or one of these organizations for more information regarding these field trials, including dates and locations of events in your area (see page 100).

Hunting Tests

Hunting tests are noncompetitive sporting events sanctioned by the American Kennel Club. For the pointing breeds, these tests first appeared back in 1986. Most are organized and run by AKC field trial clubs or by indi-

Hunting tests are fun, recreational events that both you and your dog can enjoy.

vidual breed clubs. Whereas field trials are highly competitive events that pit dog against dog for the title of "top dog," hunting tests are more laid back, with participants competing against established hunting standards rather than against other participants. The result: A recreational and relaxed event in which there is no pressure to beat the competition. Hunting tests are fun and ideal for the hobbyist who enjoys interacting with fellow bird dog owners.

Three testing or achievement levels are offered in hunting tests. These include Junior Hunter (JH), Senior Hunter (SH), and Master Hunter (MH). Each participating dog can enter (and win) at any level, yet with each successive level, the greater the refinement of hunting skills required.

Your Dog's Golden Years

As a rule, German Shorthaired Pointers are considered geriatric once they reach their seventh year (an average lifespan equals twelve years). However, just because your dog has reached a particular benchmark in years doesn't mean that the aging changes that are occurring within its body necessarily reflect those years. Genetics, nutrition, and environmental influences all ultimately affect the aging process differently in each particular individual.

It is a fact that the overall care that a dog receives throughout its life will also have a great impact upon the rate of aging. Shorthairs that have been well cared for throughout puppyhood and adult life tend to suffer fewer infirmities as they grow old than do less-fortunate canine counterparts. By practicing diligent preventative health care, the impact of many age-related health problems can be diminished.

As your Shorthair matures, it will undergo mental and physical changes resulting from years of wear and tear on all body systems. To begin, a reduction in the overall metabolic rate usually occurs, leading to reduced activity and a predisposition to weight gain. The heart becomes less efficient at pumping blood, causing an earlier onset of fatigue during exercise and hunting activities. Joint pain and reduced joint mobility may arise due to arthritis, and a general atrophy of the muscles of limbs and hips occurs due to decreased muscle activity and due to age-related protein loss from the body. As your German Shorthaired Pointer grows older, it may also experience skin and coat problems resulting from aging effects upon the hair cycle and from metabolic and endocrine upsets. The kidneys become less efficient at filtering wastes, and a decrease in liver function makes it more difficult to metabolize nutrients and detoxify poisons within the body. Fertility and reproductive performance diminish, and the incidence of uterine, mammary, and/or prostate disease increases, especially in non-neutered dogs. The gastrointestinal tract exhibits a reduced tolerance to dietary fluctuations and excesses, and the ability to digest food properly may become partially impaired, predisposing to flare-ups of gastritis, colitis, and constipation. It is well-documented that the efficiency and activity of the immune system also becomes compromised with age. As a result, geriatric pets are more susceptible to disease, especially viruses and cancer. In addition, the activity of the endocrine glands within the body may start to diminish, leaving your pet with hormone-related challenges such as hypothyroidism and diabetes mellitus. As one might expect, the aging process adversely affects mental acuity as well, which may result in noticeable senile behavior.

Finally, your dog's senses are no less susceptible to Father Time. For starters, older Shorthairs may develop a slight grayish white or bluish haze to the lenses of both eyes, termed

As your dog enters into its golden years, special care will be required.

nuclear sclerosis, or they may develop actual cataracts, the latter leading to much greater visual impairment. In addition to reduced eyesight, partial or total hearing loss is common in geriatric Shorthairs, especially those that have been exposed to gunfire for much of their lives. It is the sense of smell that is usually the last to go in older dogs. As a result, old-timers come to depend more and more on their sense of smell (rather than sight or sound) to identify people, objects, and food. Obviously, challenges in these areas can occur as this sense begins to fail. A reduced sense of smell, combined with taste-buds that don't work quite as well as they used to, can lead to finicky eating behaviors and/or reduced appetites in senior adults.

As mentioned previously, the speed at which the above changes occur will vary greatly between individual dogs, and will be affected by genetics, environment, nutrition, and by the amount of preventive health care provided. Keeping these in mind, here are a few things you can do as your dog grows older:

1. Adjust your German Shorthair's diet to match its specific health needs. For example, if your dog suffers from an age-related ailment, such as heart disease or colitis, special diets may be prescribed to reduce the wear and tear on the affected organ systems. For otherwise healthy seniors, feed a diet that is higher in fiber and reduced in calories to prevent obesity.

2. Weigh your dog on a monthly basis. Persistent weight loss or weight gain should be reported to your veterinarian.

3. Maintain a moderate exercise program for your older dog, especially during the hunting off-season. This will help keep its bones, joints, heart, and lungs conditioned. Always consult your veterinarian first as to the type and amount of exercise appropriate for your older pet.

4. Be sure to groom and brush your dog daily. Skin and coat changes secondary to aging, such as oily skin and abnormal shedding, can often be managed well with proper grooming. In addition, keep the toenails trimmed short. Older dogs suffering from arthritis don't need the added challenge and pain of having to ambulate with nails growing to the floor.

5. Semi-annual veterinary check-ups, routine teeth cleaning, and periodic at-home physical examinations for aging pets are a must. Remember: Early detection of a disease condition is the key to curing or managing the disorder. Also, because of the effects aging has on the immune system, be sure to keep your dog current on its vaccinations.

6. Be considerate of your older dog's limitations both mentally and physically. Keep food and water bowls easily accessible. Provide ramps where necessary to help the arthritic dog negotiate steps and heights. To compensate for decreased sensory awareness, approach older dogs slower than you would younger ones, using a calm, reassuring voice to further enhance recognition. Finally, be sure to give your old friend plenty of quality attention each day, continually reinforcing the companionship and bond that you two share together.

By following these tips, you can do your part to ensure that your best friend grows old gracefully and experiences golden years that are filled with nothing but health and happiness!

Useful Addresses and Literature

Registries

American Kennel Club (AKC)
5580 Centerview Drive
Raleigh, NC 27606-3390

Field Dog Stud Book (FDSB)
542 South Dearborn Street
Chicago, IL 60605

United Kennel Club (UKC)
100 East Kilgore Road
Kalamazoo, MI 49001-5598

Field Trial/Hunting Clubs and Associations

Amateur Field Trial Clubs of
America (AFTCA)
360 Winchester Lane
Stanton, TN 38069

American Bird Hunters Association
(ABHA)
510 East Davis Field Road
Muskogee, OK 74401

North American Versatile Hunting Dog
Association (NAVHDA)
P.O. Box 520
Arlington Heights, IL 60006

National Bird Hunters Association
(NBHA)
P.O. Box 1106
Van, TX 75790

National Shoot-to-Retrieve
Association (NSTRA)
226 North Mill Street, #2
Plainfield, IN 46168

U.S. Complete Shooting Dog
Association
2501 Marguerite Drive
Greensboro, NC 27406

National Breed Clubs

German Shorthaired Pointer Club of
America
1101 West Quincy
Englewood, CO 80110

National German Shorthaired Pointer
Association
P.O. Box 12263
Overland Park, KS 66212

Other Organizations

The Bird Dog Foundation, Inc.
P.O. Box 774
Grand Junction, TN 38039

Magazines and Periodicals

The American Field
542 South Dearborn Street
Chicago, IL 60605
(312) 663-9797

Gun Dog
P.O. Box 343
Mt. Morris, IL 61054
(800) 800-7724

Hunting Test Herald
51 Madison Avenue
New York, NY 10010
(212) 696-8250

German Shorthaired Pointers are an active breed.

Pointing Breed Field Trial News
51 Madison Avenue
New York, NY 10010
(212) 696-8250

The Pointing Dog Journal
P.O. Box 968
Traverse City, MI 49685
(800) 272-3246

Wing & Shot
P.O. Box 343
Mt. Morris, IL 61054
(800) 800-7724

Useful Internet Web Sites

American Kennel Club	http://www.akc.org
American Veterinary Medical Association	http://www.avma.org/home.html
Blake's GSP Cyberworld	http://looksee.com/gsp/
Canine Connections Magazine	http://www.cheta.net/connect/canine/Breeds/germshor.htm
Dog Fancy	http://www.dogfancy.com
The Dog Zone	http://www.dogzone.com/clubs/gspclub.htm
Fielddog.Com	http://www.fielddog.com/
German Shorthaired Pointer Homepage	http://www.whc.net/gsp
German Shorthaired Pointer News	http://www.geocities.com/Heartland/3960/
The Orthopedic Foundation for Animals, Inc.	http://www.prodogs.com:80/chn/ofa/index.htm
United Kennel Club	http://www.zmall.com/pet_talk/dog-faqs/kennel-clubs/UKC.html
Waltham World of Pet Care	http://www.waltham.com

Glossary

abscess: a defined collection of pus caused by a degradation of tissue.

alopecia: hair loss.

amaurotic idiocy: congenital nervous system disease in Shorthairs characterized by poor trainability, behavioral changes, and seizures.

amitriptyline HCl: an anti-anxiety medication used to treat behavioral problems in dogs.

anemia: reduction in the number of red blood cells found within the body.

anestrus: period of time in which the females ovaries are inactive.

antigen: substance capable of producing an allergic response.

ascarid: roundworm.

beneficial nematodes: special worms that can be used to control fleas in an environment.

blue eye: characteristic lesion seen in infectious canine hepatitis.

carcinogen: substance or agent capable of producing neoplastic changes in the body.

cardiovascular: pertaining to the heart and blood vessels.

cherry eye: prolapse of the gland of the third eyelid.

colitis: inflammation of the colon.

cryotherapy: treatment of neoplasia by means of applications of extreme sub-zero temperatures to freeze and kill tumor cells.

DA2LPP: abbreviation for common canine vaccine containing distemper, infectious hepatitis, leptospirosis, parainfluenza, and parvovirus antigens.

diabetes mellitus: a disease condition caused by a deficiency in the production of the hormone insulin within the body.

dietary indiscretion: the consumption of food or other substances that are not normal components of a dog's diet.

Dipylidium caninum: the common dog tapeworm.

distemper: a multisystemic disease in dogs caused by a virus.

edema: fluid retention within the tissues.

electrolyte: molecule found within body fluids that is capable of conducting an electrical current.

endocrine: pertaining to the system of hormone-producing glands found within the body.

estrogen: female sex hormone.

estrus: the period of sexual receptivity by the female; true heat.

fipronil: chemical used to kill fleas on dogs.

hard mouth: the tendency of a dog to mutilate game that it retrieves.

heartworms: parasitic worms that inhabit the heart and blood vessels of affected dogs.

heat: estrus; period of sexual receptivity.

hemostasis: the ability of the body to control internal or external bleeding.

hernia: protrusion of an organ or tissue through an opening in the body wall.

hip dysplasia: an inherited disease characterized by the malformation of the hip joints.

hookworms: parasitic worms that attach to the walls of the intestines, sucking blood and other nutrients from the host dog.

hypoglycemia: low blood sugar.

hypothermia: abnormally low body temperature.

hypothyroidism: a condition characterized by abnormally low levels of thyroid hormone within the body.

ICH (Infectious Canine Hepatitis): viral disease of dogs that adversely affects the liver, kidneys, and other internal organs.

German Shorthaired Pointers possess excellent hunting skills.

idiopathic: term used to describe any condition for which the cause is unknown.

imidacloprid: chemical used to kill fleas on dogs.

immunotherapy: treatment of neoplasia by means of immune system components.

insulin: the hormone that regulates the uptake and utilization of glucose within the body.

intradermal: within the skin.

ivermectin: an antiparasitic drug useful in preventing canine heartworm disease.

larva: an immature form of an insect.

leptospirosis: bacterial disease affecting primarily the liver and kidneys of affected dogs.

lufenuron: an insect development inhibitor used for flea control on dogs.

lumen: the interior of a hollow organ or structure.

Lyme disease: a tick-borne disease causing arthritis and other symptoms in affected dogs.

lymph: liquid substance within the body that contains immune cells, proteins, and fat molecules.

lymphedema: congenital disease characterized by puffy, swollen limbs due to an abnormal accumulation of lymph within the body.

mange: mite infestation.

mastitis: inflammation of the mammary glands.

metastasis: the spread of a tumor from its site of origin to other parts of the body.

metestrus: stage of the estrous cycle immediately following true heat.

microfilariae: heartworm larvae.

milbemycin: a drug that is used to prevent heartworm disease in dogs.

neoplasia: the abnormal growth and division of cells within the body.

neuter: to remove the ovaries and uterus in female dogs or the testicles in male dogs.

omega-3 fatty acids: fatty acids derived from cold water fish oil that are used to treat allergies and inflammation in dogs.

ophthalmic: pertaining to the eye.

otitis: inflammation of the ear.

parainfluenza: one of the organisms responsible for canine cough complex.

parturition: the birthing process.

parvovirus: infectious organism that causes severe gastrointestinal illness in affected dogs; can also lead to heart failure in puppies.

passive antibodies: protective antibodies received by a puppy in the womb or from its mother's milk.

PennHip: diagnostic procedure used to estimate the susceptibility of a dog to hip dysplasia.

polymerized borate: special powder compound used to kill fleas in the home.

proestrus: stage of the estrous cycle immediately preceding true heat.

pyrethrin: chemical used in a variety of flea sprays and shampoos; noted for its safety.

rabies: uniformly fatal viral disease transmitted primarily by the saliva of infected animals.

roundworms: parasitic worms that inhabit the lumen of the small intestine in dogs; immature forms can migrate through the tissues of the body, causing much damage.

seed ticks: tick larvae.

senses: pertaining to vision, hearing, touch, taste, and smell.

separation anxiety: abnormal behavior characterized by anxiety and stress caused by being left alone.

soft mouth: the tendency of a dog to handle retrieved game gently and to deliver it to its master unadulterated.

spay: to remove the ovaries and uterus of a female dog.

subaortic stenosis: congenital abnormality characterized by a narrowing of the vessel through which blood exits the heart and enters general circulation.

tail dock: to surgically remove a portion of or all of a tail.

tapeworms: segmented flatworms that inhabit the intestines of dogs.

testosterone: male sex hormone.

toxic-milk syndrome: syndrome affecting nursing puppies caused by tainted milk occurring secondary to mastitis.

vaginal cytology: laboratory test used to determine a female's stage of estrous.

whipworms: parasitic worms that inhabit the large intestine of infested dogs.

Index

Highly intelligent, with an incredibly strong desire to please their owners, German Shorthaired Pointers are known for their gentle dispositions and affectionate nature.